MW01232928

THE NEHEMIAH FACTORS

YOUR PATHWAY TO GODLY
EFFECTIVE LEADERSHIP

SHARON NOBUHLE WILLIAMS

GLOBAL GROWTH PUBLISHING

The Nehemiah Factors: Your Pathway To Godly, Effective Leadership
A Global Growth Factors Book

Except for those with whom expressed permission has been granted, all names are fictional to protect the parties' identities.

© 2022 by Sharon Nobuhle Williams

All rights reserved. This book is protected by the copyright laws of the United States of America. This book may not be copied or reprinted for commercial gain or profit. The use of short quotations or occasional page copying is permitted for personal or group study.

Published by Global Growth Publishing
Cincinnati, Ohio 45231.

ISBN (Paperback): 978-1-7375619-0-3
ISBN (E-book):   978-1-7375619-1-0
ISBN (Audiobook): 978-1-7375619-2-7
ISBN (Scripture Reference Guide): 978-1-7375619-3-4

Library of Congress Control Number: 2021922069

Unless otherwise noted, all Scripture quotations were extracted from the King James Version. The following abbreviations have been used to cite alternative versions of scripture:Some portions of scripture are italicized for emphasis.

AMP – The Amplified Bible - Classic Version
ASV – American Standard Version
ERV – Easy To Read Version
ESV – English Standard Version
GNB – Good News Bible
GW – God's Word
NIV – New International Version
NKJV – New King James Version
NLT – New Living Translation
WEB – World English Bible

Cover Design: Samuel Nthoroane
Editor: Paulini Turagebeci
Proofreader: Kathi Phillips

DEDICATION

I would like to dedicate this work to God, as it was He who gave it to me and inspired me to share it with you. Without Him, I would be nothing. So, Lord, I commit this project to You and thank You for choosing me to execute it. I also bless You for giving me the grace to finish, In Jesus name,

Your servant and Child,

Sharon

ACKNOWLEDGMENTS

I would like to acknowledge everyone who assisted me during the process of writing and publishing this book.

To Suffragan Bishop, David Eddings: Thank you for providing me with a living example of an effective leader. Thank you for your pastoral support, both in the US and abroad.

I would like to especially acknowledge my dear sister, Evangelist Sherri Wagner, who never allowed me to let this dream die.

I honor the late Pastor T. Alpheus Mazibuko, my host pastor, during my 2002 trip to South Africa. His ministry has impacted tens of thousands, I'm sure, and I'm only one of them. It was he who named me Nobuhle Sibusiso, a name that I've come to cherish. I'm forever grateful to his eldest daughter, Jabu, for granting my request to honor him by sharing a small snippet of my experiences with him.

I owe a debt of gratitude to all the exceptional leaders from whom I've been blessed to glean. While many were not mentioned, this book would have never made it to press without the examples they've provided through their Godly lifestyles.

To Paulini Turagabeci, my editor, and Kathy Phillips, my proofreader: Thank you for all your hard work and dedication in making this book presentable.

To all the beta readers, critique partners, and others who assisted in this project: Your help has been invaluable. Many thanks!

And finally, I would like to thank everyone else who "had my back" and encouraged me along the way. Thank you all for your prayers and support.

CONTENTS

Chapter 1

IN THE BEGINNING

In the beginning ...
(Genesis 1:1a)

THE WORDS or story of Nehemiah son of Hacaliah ...
(Nehemiah 1:1a, AMP)

J ust like creation has an origin, so does the story of Nehemiah, and so does mine. In *my* beginning, God called me to become a missionary in South Africa. Unlike the traditional scenario, He didn't assign me to a missionary program or established church with plans to travel there. God didn't move me to seek sponsorship. Instead, He gave me a vision and then instructed me to go there towards the end of 2001. I shared the vision with my pastor, who released me with his blessings. Then, in March of 2002, my journey began.

Kelly was a fellow church member who introduced herself to me after my Pastor announced that I would be traveling abroad. She asked if she could join me for a portion of the trip, and I eagerly accepted her offer. While we both served in our respective ministerial circles for years, we were new ministers zealous to serve God wherever He would send us. After two 12-hour legs aboard British Airways, we reached Johannesburg, ready to conquer the world for Christ. We arrived during the week that the Easter conferences were beginning across the country. Our host pastor, Pastor Mazibuko, arranged for us to speak at a few of the services, so we hit the ground running.

After the conferences were over, Pastor Mazibuko asked Kelly and me to present a leadership training class. The target audience was a new church that had recently elected leaders to various ministerial positions. Kelly immediately replied, "Chicken, Chicken, Chicken!" The rest of us looked at one another befuddled and began to laugh.

"So, is this the first step to effective leadership? Chicken, Chicken, Chicken," Pastor Mazibuko asked, bewildered.

Once the amusement died down, we asked Kelly why she responded that way. She said she saw a chicken restaurant's sign, and those were simply the first words to proceed from her mouth. Our attempts to understand her response created even more laughter.

When Kelly and I were alone, I asked her why she responded like that again. She told me she didn't understand why they solicited us to conduct that type of training. She said she did not feel qualified to teach such a class, so she redirected the conversation to chicken.

Kelly appeared to have quickly forgotten how God had just used us to free people from the bondage of sin while ministering at large established churches for the first time. She had forgotten how God would reveal to us precisely what issues to address at every church we ministered. From a natural perspective, her angst was justified due to our being so young in ministry. I assured her that the God who sent us had already equipped us. We only needed to put our ears to God's heart so He could show us what He would have us do.

The request didn't create unease for me. I was keenly aware of how God had been using us mightily in these unchartered waters. Still, I also wondered why they asked us to embark on such a project. I failed to realize that Pastor Mazibuko did not know my background, but he *did* know my spirit.

After Kelly returned to the States, Pastor Mazibuko asked me to conduct the training again, and I agreed. I began to listen to what God had to say regarding leadership, and He responded. The Holy Spirit instantaneously deposited several vital strategies that lay the foundation for Godly effective leadership into my spirit like a data dump. So, I conducted the training.

After the class, all of the "students" requested copies of my notes. They stated that the information I shared applied to the church world *and* the business sector. As my evangelistic tour neared its end, Pastor Mazibuko's wife also requested the notes so she could share them with their congregation. I was amazed and humbled by how God had used me.

Through this experience, God proved to me yet again that He can use anyone He wants to perform His work. He taught me that He establishes leaders despite qualifications – or the lack thereof – unlike humankind, who chooses leaders based on qualifications. He desires to equip those who are willing and obedient.

Shortly after my trip, I began reading the Book of Nehemiah. As I read, I was astounded at how Nehemiah manifested each leadership trait God had given me. That's when ***The Nehemiah Factors*** was conceived. Since then, God has led me to branch out into other topics that most people would deem me unqualified, but the messages were always well received. God then placed a series of books for me to write in my spirit covering those topics. ***The Nehemiah Factors*** is the first book in the series entitled "***Global Growth Factors.***"

In its most rudimentary state, ***Global Growth Factors*** are a variety of factors – or characteristics, traits, or lessons – designed to enhance spiritual growth individually and corporately. These factors extend beyond gender, culture, social status, politics, and geography, thus creating opportunities for spiritual growth and development globally.

This volume explores several principles that Nehemiah employed that brought him great success as a leader. In only 52 days, he transformed Jerusalem by rebuilding her walls and re-implementing reforms. Applying these principles can open the doors for your success as well. Before we take that deep dive into each principle, however, let's establish a prerequisite for this study.

Prerequisite

Gaining a foundational prerequisite is essential in leadership development. To do so, let's perform a surface study of the terms "leadership" and "principles."

Leadership:

Merriam-Webster defines a leader as: "a person who leads: as a guide, conductor and a person who has commanding authority or influence."[1] In other words, leadership means guiding people, especially by going ahead of them. To lead is to direct on a course or in a direction.

Simply put, a leader is someone who has followers. Of course, it's easy to label or categorize specific individuals who fit this description. We all recognize corporate officers, managers, pastors, school principals, and political figures as leaders. We also recognize teachers and assistants for their leading capabilities (regardless of age) because of their knowledge and awareness. But we often fail to consider parents who have a mandate to lead children into adulthood or mentors who are instrumental in encouraging and motivating protégés to achieve higher goals. When you lead someone to Christ, you do just that – lead. And let us not forget authors. If only *one* person reads this book and applies *any* of the instructions inside, I have successfully led that person.

Leadership takes on a myriad of faces, shapes, and forms. While *The Nehemiah Factors* is written from the more conventional leader's perspective, you too can benefit from this writing if you fall under any category of leadership.

Principles:

Miriam-Webster defines a principle as "a comprehensive and fundamental law, doctrine, or assumption."[2] At the most elementary level, a principle is a fundamental law that governs specific outcomes. I view principles the same way I view "if/then" statements found in mathematical equations. If "x" occurs within specific parameters, then "y" has no other option but to occur as well.

Principles govern life events on earth. God established principles in the spirit realm that extend into the natural realm. Thus, principles are spiritual in character because they are laws God implemented in heaven to lay the foundation for natural outcomes.

Sir Isaac Newton taught us several principles over which no human has control. The law of gravity is considered a natural principle that establishes that what goes up must come down.[3] Because of gravity, though airplanes can fly, they must also land.

This principle is perceived to be natural because it is usually presented in natural terms. Gravity, however, does not only exist on earth. Every mass, whether on earth or in space, has a gravitational pull.[4] Genesis 1:1 tells us that God created the heavens (plural) and the earth. In Genesis 1:8, God called the expanse above the earth "heaven." We call that "heaven" space. The degrees of gravity may vary, but gravity exists everywhere, including in space.

When the Bible states that Jesus sat down at the right hand of God in Mark 16:19, notice the Bible doesn't mention that He has to strap Himself into His throne to prevent Him from floating away. This passage reveals gravity's presence in the place where God dwells. Thus, one can deduce that the law of gravity is spiritual in nature.

Each principle illustrated in this book was created in the spirit, which causes a natural manifestation. They are Biblically-based principles at their root designed to build character. Consequently, while they apply in the church, they also evoke positive outcomes in a corporate setting.

As you read through the pages of this text, reflect on incidents where applying each principle could have changed the outcome. Then think ahead to how you can use them to alter future outcomes.

Armed with an understanding of "leadership" and "principles," let us closely examine some leadership strategies and the principles that drive them through the example Nehemiah set.

As you will discover, the book of Nehemiah is a fascinating account of courage and tenacity exhibited by one man as he walked into his God-ordained purpose. He was ordained to organize a group, rebuild a city, and rebuild the faith of its inhabitants. His story contains a treasure chest of fundamental principles and strategies that apply to anyone in a leadership position, seeking a leadership position, or assisting a leader. So, without further ado, please allow me to introduce you to Nehemiah.

Nehemiah's Story

The book of Nehemiah contains many wonderful tidbits. Here's a snippet of his journey.

As a result of evil kings ruling over Israel and Judah, the entire nation subsequently fell into captivity for 70 years. When Cyrus, king of Persia, defeated Babylon and began his rule over Judah, he permitted the Jews to return to Jerusalem and rebuild the temple. Ezra championed the temple reconstruction. Later, when King Artaxerxes of Persia took the throne, he employed Nehemiah as his cupbearer (or wine server).[5]

A wine server? Hmmm. Though it requires courage – the risk of being poisoned – how hard could that job have been? His job dictated that he pour and taste wine and food for the king to ensure it wasn't laced with poison. Yet, the role of a cupbearer was considered a very prestigious position, especially for Nehemiah, a captive foreigner.

When Nehemiah's brother told him about how bad Jerusalem had deteriorated and its effect on the Jews who returned there from captivity, Nehemiah was heartbroken. Learning about the ruined state of the wall and gates in Jerusalem was disconcerting, to say the least. Walls protected the cities from enemy invasion and attack in antiquity.[6] Without a wall, the city's inhabitants were left vulnerable and exposed. They became like sitting ducks to their enemies.

When the king noticed that Nehemiah wasn't his usual upbeat self, he asked what was wrong. Seizing the opportunity, Nehemiah shared what he had learned and requested approval to go to Jerusalem. The king granted his request and provided him with the required legal documents needed to obtain resources for the project. Nehemiah used a methodical, no-nonsense approach to rebuilding the walls. He solicited the nobles and rulers for assistance to accomplish the task and began rebuilding. He didn't allow enemy attacks to hinder their progress.

Nehemiah faced several obstacles during his rebuilding project. Yet, he rebuilt the wall and city at what some would consider lightning speed.[7]

Nehemiah appointed gatekeepers to protect the city from potential attackers and conducted a census for genealogical records. He passed the baton to Ezra, who publicly read the Law, among other things. Under Nehemiah's governorship, masses of Jews returned home and were assigned dwelling places. While Nehemiah did not rebuild the entire Judean kingdom himself, his role was pivotal in rebuilding Jerusalem.

The Kingdom of God is much the same way. Each one of us represents a part of Christ's body, and we each have a specific part to play in building God's kingdom. In addition, every role is unique and equally important.[8]

Nehemiah took his kingdom rebuilding role seriously. He was a man who walked in a spirit of excellence. Within this spirit of excellence, we find;

→ a man of Integrity,
→ a man with a Vision,
→ and a man with a Plan.

Nehemiah exhibited many leadership qualities, including:

→ Planning
→ Strategizing
→ Teamwork
→ Creating Unity
→ Problem Resolution
→ Courage, to name a few.

In *The Nehemiah Factors*, I will explore various leadership qualities Nehemiah exhibited and present the timeless usefulness of these Godly attributes today. While Nehemiah is the central player in this text, the Bible affirms the importance of confirmation on multiple occasions.[9] In that vein, I will present how Nehemiah demonstrated each principle along with other Biblical leaders to corroborate God's emphasis on each principle. I will also provide present-day evidence of each principle in action to prove its timelessness. Finally, in an endeavor to solidify the lessons of this book, each chapter will conclude with the following:

→ Key Takeaways
→ Reflections
→ Prayers

I believe it isn't enough only to be an effective leader. Many such leaders exist in the world, some who are godly, and some who are corrupt. Nevertheless, as Christians, God holds us to a higher standard. For leaders, He raises the bar even higher. Thus, the emphasis of *The Nehemiah Factors* is Godly Leadership which transitions into Spirit-Led effective leadership.

Each principle and strategy listed here is equally important. This book aims to develop leaders by building upon current strengths and improving areas of lack. Thus, I recommend that you consider reading *The Nehemiah Factors* with your Bible or *The Nehemiah Factors Scripture Reference Guide* readily accessible, to consult the vast array of scriptures referenced therein. I pray that this book will inspire you to search the scriptures for more study nuggets.

Chapter 2

THE ESTABLISHMENT PRINCIPLE

Man Qualifies, But God...

———— ～◆～ ————

...For the LORD seeth not as man seeth; for man looketh on the outward appearance, but the LORD looketh on the heart.
(1 Samuel 16:6-7)

O Lord, I beseech thee, let now thine ear be attentive to the prayer of thy servant, and to the prayer of thy servants, who desire to fear thy name: and prosper, I pray thee, thy servant this day, and grant him mercy in the sight of this man. For I was the king's cupbearer.
(Nehemiah 1:11)

I f you needed to hire someone, think for a moment about what you would look for in a potential candidate. Would you focus solely on the applicant's experience? Would you rank training as most important? Can you imagine yourself sifting through résumés to determine the person best suited for the position? If your answer to any of these questions is "yes," you are not alone.

Candidate qualifications have been an integral part of the hiring process for centuries. Hence, *The Establishment Principle* stands out more than any other because it emphasizes how much God's approach to employment differs from ours.[10]

For example, most employers base their hiring requirements on individual qualifications. Employers comb through submitted applications and résumés to find the most qualified candidate. They are searching for the answer to one simple question: "Who has the precise skill sets required to perform the duties of this position successfully?" It's all about qualifications – well ... until God is doing the hiring. When God posts a "job opening," He uses a very different set of criteria to determine the best candidate.

If I didn't know better, I'd find it quite striking that God would hire Nehemiah to fill such complex positions. While each position was managerial in nature, God was looking for one person to fill four distinct functions:

→ Project Manager
→ General Contractor
→ Union Leader
→ Governor

Nehemiah lived in the king's court of the Persian city of Susa. The only job experience listed on his résumé was that of "cupbearer," and bearing cups don't even remotely appear to equip anyone for God's job opening.[11] Yet, lacking the experience that man would require for the job, Nehemiah was 100% supernaturally equipped and capable of taking on every one of God's assignments. Thus, God chose a wine server for such a daunting undertaking.

In Matthew 22:14, Jesus said, "Many are called (job candidates), but few are chosen (hired employees)." Based on this scripture, one can assume that God called many people to do Nehemiah's job. That being the case, why in the world was Nehemiah chosen?

Here's a theory: The cupbearer position was that of a high-ranking official. The cupbearer appointment required the person to be of "irreproachable loyalty capable of winning the king's complete confidence."[12] Could that be it? ***Loyalty and faithfulness?***

God wanted someone to rebuild an entire city structure and institute reforms. Why would God choose someone seemingly so ill-equipped? Could it be that God ranks loyalty and faithfulness higher than any skill set man can bring to the table? I dare say, "Yes!" At least it's a great starting point.

Case in point: God promoted Gideon to rule Israel as a judge. God appointed him to deliver the Israelites from Midianite oppression. First, the angel of the Lord established him as a "mighty man of valor." Then, after establishing him, the Lord Himself told Gideon to use the courage He imparted into Gideon to deliver Israel from the Midianites.[13] Note that God sent the angel to establish him. The Lord Himself, however, issued the assignment without once asking for his résumé.

Gideon, however, decided to prove himself disqualified for the job. He attempted to convince God that not only was he from the weakest family in their tribe, but he was also the weakest member of his family. Even so, God didn't care about his "credentials." After Gideon sought and received signs from the Lord to confirm that God indeed had commissioned him, he accepted the "position."

When Gideon gathered his army to wage war with the Midianites, God said the army was too big and instructed him to dismiss the fearful. Then, after 22,000 men left, God told Gideon that there were still too many people. Here's where it gets strange: God then provided Gideon with instructions to ascertain whom He considered qualified. Instead of asking for a résumé, God sent them to the spring, where He proctored a simple test.

> **When Gideon led his army down to the spring, the LORD told him, "Watch how each man gets a drink of water. Then divide them into two groups—those who lap the water like a dog and those who kneel down to drink." Three hundred men scooped up water in their hands and lapped it, and the rest knelt to get a drink. The LORD said, "Gideon, your army will be made up of everyone who lapped the water from their hands. Send the others home. I'm going to rescue Israel by helping you and your army of three hundred defeat the Midianites."**
>
> **(Judges 7:5-7, CEV)**

That's right! The army that God built consisted of men willing to humble themselves and obey the order to literally lap up water like dogs.

First, God discounted the fearful because the presence of fear is the absence of faith. He doesn't want anyone who doesn't trust Him to do His bidding.

Next, He rejected the arrogant and sought out the humble. He didn't care how physically fit they were. In its very nature, humility never shows up on a résumé because the purpose of a résumé is to boast about the applicant. The 300 who lapped water were willing to humble themselves in obedience to God's command.

God dismissed the qualified and established those He hand-picked to conquer the Midianites – fearless yet humble, loyal, obedient warriors. Nehemiah exhibited these same traits demonstrated by Gideon. As you read the Book of Nehemiah, you will learn that he wielded the following characteristics:

→ Humility
→ Fearlessness
→ Loyal obedience
→ A warrior's spirit
→ Intimacy

The person best suited to fill a leadership position isn't the one with the best résumé. God-ordained leaders are spirit-led people whom God has established. They are the fearless yet humble servants willing to fight to accomplish whatever God says, no matter how ridiculous it may sound.

I can personally relate to the surprise that Gideon experienced when God chose him to lead. I've often wondered why God would select me to build a Christian Library in South Africa. Though I visited friends in South Africa a couple of times before, I knew little about South African culture.

Moreover, I knew nothing about libraries. My only relationship with libraries was checking out DVDs. While I had an extensive book collection, I don't consider myself what one would call an "avid reader." I don't even have a clue how the Dewey Decimal system works. So why me?

Most of my experience was in the telecommunications industry, which consisted of installing cables and phone equipment. I had only been in the ministry for a hot minute by this time. I had never lived outside the United States. While I had a passion for South Africa and loved to travel, I never pictured God using me in such a capacity, but God did. Jeremiah 29:11 says,

> **"For I know the thoughts that I think toward you, saith the LORD, thoughts of peace, and not of evil, to give you an expected end."**

The word "thoughts" in the King James Version is derived from the Hebrew word, *machăshebeth*, which also means plans or purposes. He lets us know that His plans will bring us to an "expected end." The "expected end" is the end God expects, or has designed for us. They are His plans for us, not our plans. God, being omnipotent, powerfully equips us to fulfill His purpose. Thus, the question becomes, what are His leadership position requirements?

Nehemiah brought humility, loyalty, courage, and intimacy to the table. He never hesitated to humble himself before God in prayer. He was loyal to the king, so it's not hard to imagine that he was also loyal to the King of kings. Faith is required to be brave enough to dedicate one's life to risk death by poison. One must trust that God will protect, creating the bravery needed for the job.

Finally, Nehemiah's intimacy with God was prevalent throughout the book of Nehemiah. He would pray at the proverbial drop of a dime (if they existed during his days, of course). He didn't care what others thought about his relationship with his God. He would boldly interact with God desiring to please Him by doing His will.

None of these traits are physical skill sets that one would put on a résumé. But since God knows our hearts' very intent,[14] He determines whom He chooses based upon what He knows about us. Once He chooses us, He then equips us to complete our assigned task. Still, it is often difficult to embrace this principle when you step into your God-given role without going through channels that society dictates.

The Establishment Issue

I recently met someone whom we will call Charity. Charity has a gift in the world of publishing, but she didn't attend your typical university majoring in publications. As a result, she didn't spend years building the perfect résumé toting a history working in major publishing houses. Yet, her eye for detail, publishing capabilities, research competence, and work ethic outshine some of the best.

Having observed Charity's gift, drive, and spirit, I sought God for His will concerning my current projects. As I considered her, I began to pray. In a previous email, I solicited her assistance. When I didn't hear back, I asked God to guide her to respond in agreement to my email if it was indeed His will for me to utilize her services. I was astounded when I finished praying and checked my messages. My inbox contained an email from her hesitantly accepting my proposal. In the email, Charity said she was reluctant because of something she referred to as the Imposter Syndrome. Having never heard of Imposter Syndrome, I did what any skilled researcher would do. I googled it.

Low and behold, my research led me to the origin of the Imposter Phenomenon. The article I found explained that many high achievers who struggle to accept their accomplishments fall prey to Imposter Syndrome. They tend to suffer from perceiving themselves as frauds.[15] Even after learning that God establishes in lieu of qualifying, Charity still mentally struggled with insecure feelings of being unqualified. Thankfully, she also said she received her breakthrough the previous night.

I can imagine that this is a common occurrence among those whom God establishes outside of normal societal channels throughout history. Take Jephthah, for example. Here you have the son of a hooker whose entire tribe sent packing. Even his sons disowned him.

He had what it took to judge Israel. Yet, the only things everyone in his orbit could see were his flaws. After that much rejection, don't you think you would suffer from Impostor Syndrome? Not Jephthah! The moment Israel found themselves fighting a leaderless war against the Ammonites, guess who came knocking? It was the very tribe that evicted Jephthah in the first place. [16] Thankfully, the potential threat of Impostor Syndrome outweighed the potential danger of the loss of freedom.

Remembering that God's hiring practices are vastly different from ours,[17] it becomes easier to understand the tendency to suffer from self-doubt. Thus, one must push past mental obstacles and embrace God's assignment to experience the thrill of fulfilling His will.

My Establishment

Before my trip abroad, I had traveled internationally multiple times, including two previous trips to South Africa, so I had become a bit familiar with the culture. I am also an authorized instructor in Ministering Spiritual Gifts,[18] so I scheduled a series of meetings with Kelly to help her prepare for the journey spiritually and culturally. Since we had only recently met, I felt that these meetings would also provide an opportunity for us to get to know one another.

During one of our meetings, Kelly told me that she asked God why I would be the one developing her. She explained that in her mind, it should have been the other way around. Kelly pointed out that she had only seen me at church for a few years, but she had been in church her entire life. Kelly had created a mental résumé of what she thought were my capabilities based on her limited knowledge of me, but God chose me based on the intent of my heart. Then, He equipped me. Like many others have done, she attempted to qualify me, but God had already established me.

God gave me the vision to build a Christian Library in South Africa one day in 2001 while I was driving. As I listened to gospel music, I saw the vision of a boy in a tent reading a book. Immediately I heard the Lord speak into my spirit to build a Christian library. He even gave me the name of the project: The South African Spiritual Development Project. For someone who very rarely sees visions, it didn't take rocket science for me to figure out that He chose me – someone who knew no more about libraries than how to check out DVDs!

As soon as I reached my destination, I immediately wrote what the Lord had placed into my spirit. I presented it to my pastor, and six weeks later, there I was in South Africa attending services – both large and small – in tents, among other places. Incidentally, when I saw the vision, I had no idea that most churches in South Africa fellowshipped in tents, except for a few mega-churches. One day while there, I felt led by the Holy Spirit to share a personal trial with Kelly that God had brought me through soon after becoming a Christian.

On the evening that The Lord filled me with the Holy Spirit, in the spring of 1980, I was so elated that I couldn't wait to tell my mother the great news. Exactly one week earlier, I let her talk me into attending the church she had visited. I had no interest in going, but Mommy just wouldn't shut up about it. Bright and early the following morning, we headed to church. It was the first service

I attended in years. *Boy, this woman knows how to torture people,* I thought.

Well, I heard about someone that day. His name was Jesus. I didn't realize it until almost a week later, but He had already begun a work in me. The following Saturday, I visited a neighbor who laid hands on me in prayer. That prayer was instrumental in transforming my entire life. As I praised God, I could physically feel the Holy Spirit enter my body as I simultaneously began speaking in tongues. As I inhaled, it felt as if a strong burst of air – akin to breath someone receiving CPR would inhale – entered from my mouth and flooded my very core. I had literally experienced what the disciples experienced in Acts 2:1-4. To say that the joy I was experiencing was palpable is an understatement.

Unfortunately, within 24 hours, my mother was manic. Every day after that was fraught with turmoil. A few weeks later, we had to have her committed to the psychiatric ward. So began a 10-year cycle of commitment and release.

I'll never forget that Mother's Day when my entire church witnessed her mania in action. She was so disruptive that the ushers escorted her out of the sanctuary through one of the two exit doors. The disruption continued until well after service ended. She refused to leave, forcing the other attendees to leave the sanctuary via the other exit door. Imagine being an 18-year-old at a service consisting of more than 1,500 people as they watch your mother experiencing a mental breakdown!

During one of her episodes, I couldn't bear the pressure, so I left home. A couple of days later, the saga continued as my father had her committed again. While my mother and my sister, Gail, were at a friend's house, the police arrived and began to rough my mother up. Gail asked them why they had to be so rough. The police's answer was to handcuff and arrest Gail. By the time I arrived at my house, my father was in hysterics. "They arrested my baby," he cried. I had never seen him cry before, and since tears are highly contagious, I commenced to cry as well.

First, we stopped to catch our collective breath. Then we dried our tears and headed to the courthouse, the bail bondsman, to breakfast to wait until Gail was processed, then back to the courthouse. Seeing Gail behind the glass with her head hung, appearing dejected as she waited to be processed, brought him to tears again as we entered the courthouse.

Our family carried this burden for the next ten years until a physical illness claimed my mother's life. I did not realize that I didn't know what struggles were until this experience. But God anointed me to endure it and graced me to come out unscathed and with a more intimate relationship with Him. Had it not been for the Holy Spirit residing in me, comforting me, leading and guiding me, I have no idea how I would have endured the trauma. God did not allow this series of events to destroy me. He allowed them to strengthen and equip me for the future He had in mind for me.

Less than a year after the ordeal began, I visited a friend's father in the hospital. I didn't say much during the visit, but I was stunned by what he *did* say. "You have become quite patient," he surmised. I didn't know that God was busy preparing me way back then for where he would take me decades later.

I'll never forget Kelly's reaction when I finished the story. "You never know the things people have been through," she said, shaking her head dumbfounded. I only shared a fraction of my journey with her. She had no idea of what trials I'd overcome. She didn't know the battles I fought. At that moment, however, she rewrote her mental résumé of me that she had previously created. I believe that's when she began to understand that God established me "for such a time as this."[19]

When God called Jeremiah – the "weeping" prophet – into the prophetic ministry, He said,

> **"Before I formed you in the womb I knew [and] approved of you [as My chosen instrument], and before you were born I separated and set you apart, consecrating you; [and] I appointed you as a prophet to the nations."**
>
> **(Jeremiah 1:5, AMP)**

God established Jeremiah before he was born to be a prophet. Likewise, He established me to be a missionary before my parents conceived me. Discounting God's input when employing a potential candidate may create a roadblock to the success of a project or program. So, next time you presume to judge someone as unqualified to lead in the capacity you think they can, think again. That "someone" may just be you.

Key Takeaways:

→ God's process of selecting candidates for His "job openings" is not based on man's pre-conceived notions but rather on one's willingness to heed His call. Those He calls, He also equips.

→ God established Nehemiah because he was a fearless yet loyal and obedient warrior who had an intimate relationship with Him. These are the requirements God uses to determine those that He will establish.

→ When someone inappropriately judges another person as unqualified, the ability to discern God's chosen candidate becomes blocked.

Reflection:

→ Were there ever times in your life that you were given a responsibility for which you felt ill-equipped?

→ Were you able to manage that responsibility successfully despite the lack of training or experience?

→ Name three areas to which you can apply The Establishment Principle in your life.

Prayer:

Dear heavenly Father, I thank you for establishing and equipping me to fulfill Your will here on the earth. Please grant me wisdom and grace to tap into the equipment You've placed inside me so that I can boldly declare Your glory through the demonstration of my work in Your kingdom. I ask this in Jesus' mighty name. AMEN!

Chapter 3

THE FOUNDATION PRINCIPLE

Seek Ye First

One thing have I desired of the LORD, that will I seek after; that I may dwell in the house of the LORD all the days of my life, to behold the beauty of the LORD, and to enquire in his temple.
(Psalm 27:4)

... I beseech thee, O LORD God of heaven, the great and terrible God, that keepeth covenant and mercy for them that love him and observe his commandments:
(Nehemiah 1:5)

Sometimes I feel like my mind is organized like a big bowl of spaghetti. I most often recognize this feeling of internal chaos when starting new projects. Whether I'm writing articles, preparing messages, or forming a library program, I must first unravel any new undertaking like that bowl of spaghetti – one noodle at a time. If I don't, my brain breaks. The only way to repair my brain is to implement *The Foundation Principle* by seeking God for divine direction.

Nehemiah provides us with a glimpse into the inner workings of *The Foundation Principle.* He received word about how the Jews who escaped captivity and returned to Jerusalem suffered in Nehemiah chapter one. Upon learning that the city's wall and gates were in ruins, his reaction was to intercede continually.[20]

And I said, "O LORD God of heaven, the great and awesome God who keeps covenant and steadfast love with those who love him and keep his commandments, let your ear be attentive and your eyes open, to hear the prayer of your servant that I now pray before you day and night for the people of Israel your servants, *confessing the sins of the people of Israel, which we have sinned against you.* Even I and my father's house have sinned. We have acted very corruptly against you and have not kept the commandments, the statutes, and the rules that you commanded your servant Moses. Remember the word that you commanded your servant Moses, saying, 'If you are unfaithful, I will scatter you among the peoples, but if you return to me and keep my commandments and do them, though your outcasts are in the uttermost parts of heaven, from there I will gather them and bring them to the place that I have chosen, to make my name dwell there.' They are your servants and your people, whom you have redeemed by your great power and by your strong hand. O Lord, let your ear be attentive to the prayer of your servant, and to the *prayer of your servants who delight to fear your name, and give success[21] to your servant today, and grant him mercy in the sight of this man."*

(Nehemiah 1:5-11, ESV, emphasis added)

In his distress, Nehemiah's focus shifted directly to the only One who could exact a change. He understood that it was all about God and His divine plan to remedy the situation. He recognized that without God, he was nothing. As we read his prayer, we discover that he had already pondered the problem and formulated a plan. Holding God to His promise, he then proceeded to seek God for the mercy of the king, thus applying *The Foundation principle*.

Jesus brought *The Foundation Principle* to light when he said,

Seek ye First the Kingdom of God, and his righteousness; and all these things shall be added unto you.

(Matthew 6:33)

Nehemiah must have known that he had a responsibility beyond intercession. Thus, his prayer for mercy in the sight of the king. Yet, when his opportunity to present his case before the king arose, the Bible says he was "sore afraid." That doesn't sound like a little nervous to me.

While he was serving the king, the king confronted him concerning his countenance. Why was he so scared? Did he fear rejection? Or, did he fear for his very freedom or life? Nehemiah knew that mourning was forbidden in the king's presence. He also knew that it was dangerous for someone in his position to ask an audience of the king, let alone appear sorrowful.[22] This man was petrified, and fear "brings with it the thought of punishment."[23] Was he fearful of the king's judgment?

Regardless of the origin of Nehemiah's fear, he proceeded to present the matter to the king. When King Artaxerxes asked what Nehemiah wanted from him, Nehemiah immediately consulted his True King – The Lord God Jehovah in prayer before responding. Regardless of our circumstances, we must learn to take all our matters before our King. Keeping them from Him will only impede, if not rob, us of our breakthrough or success.

Nehemiah could identify the problem in his mind's eye. God had given him clear insight while he consecrated himself. As a result, he was physically, mentally, and emotionally equipped to walk in God's purpose for his life. Hence, as he wrote what I'm sure is a minute portion of his prayers, his requests were specific: Forgiveness, favor, and mercy with the king.

Of these requests, favor clearly reflects that he already decided to do something to rectify the situation. The Bible does not disclose what he had in mind at that time, but Nehemiah knew he had a mandate to exact a change at some level. He refused to sit idly by and gripe. Instead, he became an active and willing participant, a doer of the word that God had given him, not a hearer only.[24]

Nehemiah's prayer was his way of acknowledging God in his decision and seeking divine direction. The result of his applying **The Foundation Principle** by seeking God first was made evident by Artaxerxes granting all of his requests. He sought the Kingdom of God, and *"all these things,"* i.e., everything he needed to embark on his assigned task, was added to him.[25]

Critical leadership arenas in which prayer is of paramount importance include:

→ Plan development

→ Structure creation

→ Battle preparation (i.e., equipping oneself for overcoming obstacles)

→ Sharpening of spiritual senses through increased intimacy

Divine Plans and Decisions

When God showed me that He had plans for me to serve ministerially in South Africa, He showed me a specific task, but not all the details. Filled with zeal, I quickly began formulating my plan. Shortly afterward, I found myself visiting South Africa for two and a half months. Yet, the work had not started. I had no idea that it would be another six years of continual intercession and a willingness to literally let go of all my possessions before I could witness the vision become a reality. I had to surrender every plan I made to Him totally, and boy, were His plans far different from mine.

After my trip in 2002, I envisioned spending six months per year in South Africa and six months at home. While I was there, I remember a pastor showing me a vacant bank building suggesting that it would be ideal for a Christian library. Of course, I added that to my list. My plans included things like complete autonomy and the freedom to move about the country at will. Then, when I became tired of not enjoying all the comforts of home, I'd head back to the USA to regroup and refresh myself. That's how I saw my journey unfold. Those were my plans. Not God's.

When I came back to the States, I eagerly developed a checklist of everything I thought I needed to implement God's plan. Whenever an idea popped into my head, I'd find myself hunting down my Palm Pilot to ensure that it made my list. For the next six years, I laid those plans before the Lord, but one by one, the doors began to shut until finally, I surrendered them all to His will.

One example concerned transportation. I couldn't envision accomplishing God's mission without a car, so of course, that was at the top of my list. As it turned out, I didn't need a car after all, but that didn't stop me from attempting to obtain a South African driver's license in preparation. I arrived with an international driver's license, which lasted for one year. I only had a few opportunities to drive since I didn't own a car, in any case. Yet, I didn't learn my lesson.

One day after the international license expired, I continued to force my will when I arrived outside the License Bureau at around 5 AM to take the written exam. The lines were so long that arriving any later could prove to be an unfruitful trip. Slowly the line moved until I finally found myself at the entrance gate a few hours later. The security guard on duty handed me a slip of paper with a pre-scheduled appointment for a later date to take the written exams.

Upon returning for my appointment, the first hurdle I faced was an eye exam. Boy, was that a surprise! I could barely see out of my Dollar Store readers, and the Coke bottles that substituted themselves for distance glasses were also subpar. So there I was, pressing my eyes against the machine, having no clue what I was looking for or where it was. Just as the not-so-happy clerk was attempting to fail me, I quickly said, "Wait! Let me switch glasses." But, of course, they were no better. Her impatience worked in my favor, nonetheless. Unwilling to put up with my stall-tactics any longer, she handed me a begrudging pass as she gave a sideways glance to her co-worker.

After illegitimately passing the vision test, I took the written exam. Amazingly, I passed and collected my learner's permit. Did I ever use it? Not once, and I never had an opportunity to take the actual driver's test. SLAM! One of many doors shut just like that, but God had His reasons. First, He knew how dangerous it could be for a lone female traveler, especially a foreigner. Second, God desired that I fully immerse myself in South African culture.

My first cultural lesson was learning to use public transport. It was like no other experience I've had, but I mastered it. In time, I even became almost proficient with counting the money, calculating, and passing back change for the driver when sitting in the front. Trust me. It was no easy feat.

The taxi will not leave the rank until it is completely full – up to 15 passengers crammed together like sardines. Having long legs, I learned from experience that I should attempt to sit in the front at all costs. While that seat provided much-needed legroom, it came with a grave responsibility. As soon as the driver would leave the rank, someone would gently press on my shoulder to pass money to me. That person would say something like, "Fifty Rand four," – which means they are giving me R50 to pay for the four passengers in one of the rows.

Without a calculator, I must multiply the fare by four, subtract the total from R50, and pass back the change. While I'm figuring out how much change to send back, another press on the shoulder – another row of paying customers – would interrupt my calculations. Of course, that's not such an arduous task when the fare is R10. But Nooooooo.

The fare on my taxis was always something like R8.25. So now, here I am, busy trying to figure out what each funny colored note and weirdly shaped coins were when someone would press my shoulder again. Of course, this time, it would be a different amount for a different number of people. Oh. By the way, did I mention that the taxis contained at least four rows? Needless to say, by the time someone pressed on my shoulder the fourth time, I would feel like the only way to accomplish my assigned task was to count in tongues. Oh yeah,

and did I forget to tell you that math in tongues isn't necessarily the best form of calculation?

Even though the passenger in front having to collect fares is an unspoken rule, drivers often let me off the hook. Either they felt sorry for me, or they just couldn't trust me with their hard-earned money. I know I wouldn't trust me. Although eventually, I began to adapt.

As my ministry-related responsibilities increased, public transport became cumbersome. Thus, my dear friend, sister Tozamile Mqhum became my self-appointed driver. She was usually only a phone call away and the perfect travel companion throughout South Africa and Botswana. After the unnecessary battle of attempting to obtain a car, God proved that He would be faithful to provide everything I needed.

Surrendering totally to God's will resulted in what would become the best six years of my life. The future He expected for me was far greater than I could have ever imagined.[26] I had to lay all my plans before Him, however, to determine if they were aligned with His will. My life became much more abundant once I surrendered them to Him and submitted to His divine plan.[27]

Do you have a God-given dream that seems may never come to pass? Have you ever embarked upon a project only to ultimately abandon it? These scenarios are sadly all too common. Typically, this happens when we get ahead of God's plan. He will often show us the big picture simply to give a glimpse of the outcome. This outcome is the final destination, not the entire roadmap. Without His roadmap (the "who, what, when, where, why, and how"), we may find our efforts to fulfill vision ineffective at best.

God's instructions to Noah to build the ark provide us with a complete roadmap.[28] The "who" was Noah's family and all the animals he accommodated. The "what" were the materials he needed to build the ark and exact measurements. The "when" and "where" were literally right then and there, as urgency was in the air. The rains fell only seven days after completion. The "why" was because the corrupt pervasiveness of sin had polluted the population. The "how" was in the architectural design God provided Noah. Even the exact time they would enter the ark was spelled out. Noah did not enter the ark until God instructed him to do so – again, the "when."

Often when we become established in a position and begin to get an idea of what we are doing, we assume we **know** what we are doing. We then often start acting based upon what we **think** we know without first consulting God. By contrast, God orders the steps of a good man.[29] Not just the first step, but all of the steps. He teaches us through Proverbs 3:4-5 to:

Trust in the LORD with all thine heart; and lean not unto thine own understanding. In all thy ways acknowledge him, and he shall direct thy paths.

When we bring every idea and issue before God first and allow Him to guide us, our spiritual eyes become focused on a more precise direction. Our job is to build God's Kingdom regardless of our area of expertise. This mandate applies to leading church groups, developing community enrichment programs, or marketplace ministry.[30]

Why do I begin with laying plans before God? A plan is required to execute a project successfully. A plan provides the structure necessary to attain any goal. With that in mind, let's consider the importance of structure.

From Chaos to Structure

According to Merriam Webster, the transitive verb definition of structure is to set in a logical order,[31] which is precisely what Nehemiah did. By chapter three, Nehemiah has enjoyed God's favor via King Arterxerxes after seeking God for guidance. Per his request, the king then sent him to Jerusalem to oversee the project.

Nehemiah chapter three continues the story with a type of organization chart that explains each group in Nehemiah's team, their roles, and responsibilities. He knew their gifts, strengths, weaknesses, and skill sets. He knew that Eliashib was a high priest, which qualified him to sanctify the sheep gate. He knew that the nobles of Tekoa were not qualified to do the work of their superiors, so they were only assigned to do repairs. He also knew everyone's boundaries.

As a result, he ensured that there was structure within Team-Jerusalem. His organization chart clearly defined the structure built into Nehemiah's plans. Applying structure to our plans is crucial. Structure brings about the following:

→ Form
→ Balance
→ Order
→ Discipline

When I first moved into my house in Arizona, I had a water softener system installed in the hall closet. Eleven years later, it began to leak. When the plumbing company removed it, they failed to cap the water pipes properly. At around 5:00 A.M. the following morning, I awoke to a gushing sound. When I stepped out of my bed, my feet landed in a puddle of water. I went to the hall closet to discover that the pipes were spewing water like a broken dam. The water covered everything in its path, causing thousands of dollars in water damage.

My insurance adjuster alerted me of the urgency of turning off the main water valve. She said the water level would have exceeded the electrical outlets at the rate that the water was flowing from the pipe, significantly increasing the damage and creating a fire hazard. It was the formlessness of the water that wreaked havoc in my home.

When God created the heavens and the earth in Genesis chapter 1, He created structure. The first thing we see in the creation story is water, a formless and disruptive substance. Water in and of itself has no structure. It is a liquid mass that, without boundaries, engulfs everything around it. The formlessness of water is what makes it destructive. Without form (or structure), we only have chaos, hence the need for plans.

God's first order of business was to hover over the waters. He evaluated the current condition and executed His plan. He started by creating light.[32] For without light, just like water, the formlessness of darkness will engulf all objects in its path. Unseen objects can be dangerous weapons. For example, a rusty nail protruding from the grass can puncture one's foot.

God created light first to set boundaries for darkness. Once the waters were made visible by the light, He set limits for the water by creating the sky. Next, he commanded the submerged land to appear.[33] Any project, task, or mission without structure has the potential of being swallowed up in the chaos that formlessness creates. By creating boundaries for darkness and water, God established structure on the earth. He built structure using a step-by-step plan of action consisting of:

1. Surveying the conditions
2. Creating light
3. Creating the sky
4. Exposing land by setting boundaries for the waters[34]

As we continue reading the book of Nehemiah, we discover that Nehemiah followed in God's footsteps by surveying the conditions first. He then brought light to the city's current circumstances with the community leaders.[35] Next, Nehemiah took advantage of the daylight hours to diligently work until they completed the project. Finally, he culminated his work by setting boundaries between the inhabitants of the land and their enemies.

Proverbs 21:5 (ESV) tells us that "The plans of the diligent lead surely to abundance." Nehemiah did just that. By submitting his plans to God for divine direction, Nehemiah reaped the reward of absolute success. When you yield your plans to the Lord and surrender to His plans for you, expect two things:

1. An abundance of resources will become available to you.
2. The success you imagined will become accessible.[36]

When I completely surrendered my so-called "missions" plans to God, I didn't expect Him to tell me to get rid of all my possessions. In 2008, during the height of the housing crisis, I felt as if my house was the last major blessing that He had allowed me to keep up to that point, so when He told me to sell it, I was shaken to my core. Anxiety flooded my very being as I obediently consulted with my real estate agents.

They told me not to expect it to sell for at least a year. No house had been sold in my neighborhood in the two years prior. Ironically though, the minute they staked the "For Sale" sign into the front yard, unspeakable joy instantly replaced the anxiety. The fact that I had no idea where I would be staying, what I would be doing, or how I would support myself financially had no bearing on the joy I experienced.

Three weeks later, I sold my house for the exact asking price. A few weeks after that, I found myself flying to the O. R. Thambo International Airport in Johannesburg. God had opened His reservoir of resources to me. He supplied me with accommodations and all other necessities required to fulfill His will for me throughout my entire stay.

My greatest enemy during those six years was my mind. Confronting anxiety, doubt, and fear was a continual battle. Fortunately, however, God fortified me with His spiritual weapons as described in Ephesians 6:10-17 to stave off an emotional shipwreck. Thus, He thoroughly equipped me for the battle.

Let's Get Ready to Rumble

In Nehemiah chapter 4, Sanballat, a Moabite who held office under the Persian government, began taunting the Jews who were repairing the wall.[37] Nehemiah intervened by asking God to avenge him of his enemies. Take note of his petition during his conversation with God.

> *Hear, O our God; for we are despised: and turn their reproach upon their own head, and give them for a prey in the land of captivity: And cover not their iniquity, and let not their sin be blotted out from before thee: for they have provoked thee to anger before the builders.*
>
> *(Nehemiah 4:4-5)*

The story then shows Nehemiah and his cohorts armed and ready for a physical battle.[38] Nehemiah recognized, however, that they could not win the physical battle until he set the stage in the spirit realm through prayer. He realized that weapons of our warfare are not natural,[39] so we must learn how to fight in the spirit realm. Events in the physical realm are nothing more than a reaction to what is happening in the spirit realm.[40] To exact a change in our physical lives, we must tap into the spirit realm through prayer.

In Nehemiah chapter 6, Nehemiah sought God to avenge him of his adversaries once again. Nehemiah spoke in the spirit realm to reverse the curse that Sanballat and Tobia, an Ammonite married to a Jewess, attempted to place upon him through their words.[41] They sent messengers to Nehemiah repeatedly, endeavoring to schedule a meeting with them to convince him to stop working. He rejected their petitions, so they sent a letter to the king. In the letter, they accused Nehemiah of rebelling against Persia and attempting to appoint himself as king of Judah, "so I suggest that you come and talk it over with me," Sanballat wrote.[42] Nehemiah sent word back to Sanballat that they were flat-out liars, and he would not succumb to their feeble attempts. Sanballat and Tobia then attempted to curse their work by saying, "their hands shall be weakened from work."

Nehemiah apparently understood that "death and life are in the power of the tongue."[43] Therefore, he proceeded to reverse the curse they pronounced through their words by speaking into the atmosphere when he petitioned God to do the opposite: "strengthen my hands." After his simple prayer, he continued with business as usual, none the weaker.

During our 2002 South African trip, Pastor Mazibuko organized various meetings for us to minister. During Easter weekend, there were a variety of conferences taking place. We were not slated to preach anywhere on Sunday, so we attended the meeting held at the church that Pastor Mazibuko attended. I arrived at the service with Kelly and Pastor Ramakarane – who opened the doors of his home to accommodate us –and settled in. Shortly after the service started, however, someone told me that I must leave to speak at a different conference. Someone then dropped me off at the other service and left me there alone.

Immediately upon arriving, I began to intercede for the service and seek God for what message He wanted me to deliver. As the service started, I continued praying. Instantly, God alerted me that I didn't have my camcorder with me. Nevertheless, I felt it was vital that we record the service. Realizing there was no way I could physically communicate with anyone at the original service, I began to seek God for guidance. Through His prompting, I turned to the spirit realm.

Jesus, who took on human form and walked this earth like every other man, spoke to Lazarus' spirit four days after he died. He didn't go into Lazarus' tomb, nor did He pray to the Father. He simply said, "Lazarus, come forth."[44]

Armed with that reminder and the promise that we would do greater works,[45] I spoke softly to Pastor Ramakarane's spirit right from my seat, knowing full well that he was currently at the original service. "Pastor Ramakarane, please bring me my camcorder in Jesus' name," I whispered, then shifted my attention back to the worship service.

About fifteen minutes later, I looked up, and who was approaching me? None other than Pastor Ramakarane himself, in the flesh. In addition to my camcorder, He also brought the gentlemen who recorded all the services I ministered in. Excited, I told him I had forgotten my camcorder. He replied, "I know. That's why I've come." He then dropped off the camcorder and my "media guy" and returned to his service.

Later, when sharing the story with Kelly, she said she was sitting beside him during their service at the exact time I spoke into the spirit realm. She looked at him and observed him silently praying. Then all of a sudden, his eyes popped open, and he said in a panic, "Oh my goodness! Sister Sharon's camcorder!" He then jumped up and left.

Pastor Ramakarane later told me that he had to drive from the service he attended to his house (about a 15-minute drive) and then to me (another 15-minute drive). We ascertained that what should have taken him 30 minutes only took 15. It appeared that God also supernaturally condensed the time for me[46] to ensure that I was provided for and that my prayer was answered.

Earlier, I quoted Proverbs 18:21, which says

Death and life are in the power of the tongue.

What we say affects what happens both naturally and spiritually. Words *are* spirit. They produce life or cause death. Thus, speaking into the spirit realm can impact seemingly large and small matters alike. Imagine how much you can conquer when you confront situations by exercising your spiritual authority? Jesus gave us the power to loose and bind on earth *and* in heaven.[47] So, let's begin loosing the blessings that will usher us into vision fulfillment and binding the curses that have hindered us from realizing our destinies.

Come, Let's Reason

The keys to the kingdom that Jesus promised to Peter granted him the power to loose and bind.[48] We activate the same power in the spirit realm through prayer, which exacts changes in the earth. When we pray, we communicate directly with God. Paul reminded us to:

Pray without ceasing. (1 Thessalonians 5:17)

Prayer is also a tool that helps us sharpen our spiritual senses.[49] Through our communication with God, our level of intimacy with Him increases. As our intimacy grows, we inherit a clearer understanding of His direction.

When you seek God in your team selection process, for example, you may find that your chosen group will collectively share your vision. Some candidates may not appear qualified according to man's standards. Nevertheless, using divine guidance in the selection process guarantees that they will be fully equipped to carry out the vision.

I once asked a successful cell group[50] leader how he establishes them. He responded, "through prayer meetings." Several of his cell groups became churches.

In Luke 18, we find Jesus sharing the parable of an unjust and irreverent judge. An ill-treated widowed woman sought him to punish those who wronged her. Initially, he disregarded her request. Then, after he pondered the matter, he felt she would bug him to death if he didn't avenge her of her adversaries. His *reasoning* caused him to grant her request speedily. Through that parable, Jesus is teaching us a key ingredient concerning our prayer life: continual intercession. While it isn't necessary to beg God, we mustn't hesitate to consistently go before God and make our petitions known before Him.[51]

I once heard Creflo Dollar say, "when you seek God, things will find you. If you seek His face first, you'll receive what is in His hands." I have found this to be true in my personal life. When God guided me into full-time ministry in 2001, I had a great job making an enviable salary, but I didn't have the luxury of any other income. I worked in telecom for about 15 years when the industry suffered a catastrophic decline.[52] Little did I know that God would soon share with me the ministerial goals He had in mind for me.

Around this time, the telecommunications industry was thrust into a crisis because of Lucent Technologies' books-cooking schemes. That crisis left our company battered and struggling. I was ready to leave the industry and had contemplated quitting. Then, a few months later, my manager called me into her office to notify me that the company was laying me off.

I knew I could live comfortably making half my salary, so I began pondering what I would like to do next as I drove home. I wanted a complete change. I was bored by Telecom and wanted to take time off to weigh my options. I decided I wouldn't even pray about what I would do next until I knew what I wanted specifically. By the time I reached my house, I had decided that a nap was more important since I hadn't slept enough before heading to work that morning.

There I lay on my bed with my eyes closed, patiently awaiting the arrival of Lala-land, but my mind just wouldn't shut up. I began picturing myself in what I considered my "dream job." As a visual began to form, I realized that everything in my mind's eye pointed to ministry. Then, the Lord said, "What about full-time ministry?" Being new to ministry, this was the furthest thing from my mind.

This question knocked my eyes right back into the open position. I immediately considered how the churches I fellowshipped in didn't provide financial compensation to many of their ministers. So much for my nap. I stared into my open closet in stunned silence. Knowing God's voice, however, I knew that He knew what was best for me. So, I reasoned with Him. I said, "Well, Your word says, 'I've never seen the righteous forsaken, nor his seed begging for bread,' and 'I can do all things through Christ who strengthens me.'[53] So, if You promise to take care of me and mine" – my house and car since my "mine" didn't include family – "I'll do it."

I struggled with one dilemma, however. I was torn between the scripture that says, "if a person doesn't work, don't let him eat," and "to obey is better than sacrifice."[54] I had to examine what "work" truly means in God's mind. I didn't understand that God was hiring me to work for Him directly in return for His provisions. Nonetheless, I decided that I would accept His job offer. Little did I know that I would find myself on my first trip as a missionary less than a year later.

I recently read an article written by Kathy Howard. In the article, she shared an experience her children had with a raft in a swimming pool. The raft was eventually punctured and no longer served its purpose, so she threw it away. Of the boat, she wrote, "It was supposed to be in the water, but the water was not supposed to be in the boat.[55]

Often, by being "in" the world, we tend to subscribe to the world's systems because of visibility. But this mindset can derail us from God's agenda for us. Few people regard God's work as "real" work because God's pay system isn't the same as the world's. My obedience to God's guidance created an atmosphere of rejection and ridicule. Only a handful of people understood my decisions at that time, but I had to trust that God would keep His promise. In the process of time, my savings dwindled. Only then did I learn what actual reliance on God meant, as I never suffered lack.

It was vital for me to push past the ridicule and reject the naysayers' reports, those very things that could provoke me to disobedience. I had to note that when my well ran dry or when it seemed I was drowning, God would send "things" to find me. First, money would find its way into my hands, as people would give into my "bosom."[56] The "holy handshake" – the act of pressing cash into someone's hand while shaking hands – became a pleasant occurrence.

Next, the first "job" found me when my karate instructor asked if I would consider conducting Defensive Drivers classes for his Driving School. Importantly, it did not rob me of my focus on ministry as it only required my attention a couple of times per month. Then, when that well began to run dry, the second job, as a telecommunications technician, came knocking at my door. While these two jobs had nothing to do with my calling, they provided me with much-needed finances and the flexibility to focus on ministry for that season.

When the second job threatened to encroach on God's job, God dropped the third job in my lap, with no strings attached. This job came with the added perk of travel. For 12 months, I commuted from Phoenix to El Paso, Texas to care for an aged pastor and his wife. While the position itself was not ministry, it was directly tied to my future in missions. God graced me with direct access to the pastor's wisdom as I provided care for the lovely couple. I would later tap into that wisdom during my journeys.

It was indeed a new beginning for me of sorts, something I had to continually remind myself when noting that none of those jobs appeared to propel me forward. Those jobs existed to keep me from drowning. They kept me walking on water, holding my Master's hand.[57]

I'm not promoting that those in need of employment or finances do nothing in the name of seeking to realize their dreams. Nor is my goal to discourage anyone from pursuing financial stability, as faith without works is dead.[58] I am simply stressing the importance of seeking God first and trusting Him to fulfill His promise of allowing "all these things to be added."[59] My goal is to encourage you to pursue what God instructed you to pursue. Will what you are seeking help you reach your destiny or drive you away from it? The answer will point you in the right direction.

Let us seek His face for what we need. Let us surrender everything to God and allow Him to give us the wisdom to perform what He would have us do efficiently. In doing so, we can rest assured that vision will become a reality.

Key Takeaways:

→ Seeking God's kingdom and righteousness through continued intercession is the first and most important priority when embarking on any new endeavor. In doing so, you lay a solid, unshakeable foundation for that endeavor.

→ Distinguishing between God's plans and yours is vital in successfully launching and maintaining your assignment.

→ Structure is compulsory for launching and maintaining a meaningful mission. God's creation provides us with a perfect illustration for laying an organized foundation.

Reflections:

→ Ponder and document a time (or times) where you discovered that your plans were not the same as God's plans for you. How did (or can) you rectify those mistakes?

→ Define three areas of your life that need to be structured or restructured.

→ How will you implement structure to the areas that you have identified?

Prayer:

Gracious Lord, please forgive me for those times that I've forgotten to seek You first when beginning a new undertaking. Thank You for empowering me with the knowledge that You are patiently awaiting my audience. I come to You now seeking divine direction, resources, and wisdom to fulfill Your will. Please give me clarity of mind and purpose. Give Your servant ears to hear Your voice clearly, a heart to receive Your word fully, and a mind to obey Your instructions completely. I praise You in advance for Your forgiveness and answers. This I pray, in Jesus' name, AMEN!

Chapter 4

THE PRIORITIZATION PRINCIPLE

... And then ...

For precept *must* be upon precept, precept upon precept; line
upon line, line upon line; here a little, *and* there a little: For with
stammering lips and another tongue will he speak to this people.
(Isaiah 28:10-11)

Then I commanded, and they cleansed the chambers: and thither
brought I again the vessels of the house of God, with the meat offering
and the frankincense... And I gathered them together, and set them
in their place... And I made treasurers over the treasuries...
(Nehemiah 13:9-13)

When I worked as a technician for Lucent Technologies, I installed telephone systems for businesses. Many of these companies were startups or moving to new locations. Thus, the jobs were often split into phases: cable installation, system installation, and training. By the time we would arrive to install the cables, the building's shell, electrical wires, pipes, and roof were already installed. Often, the electricity was on, and insulation was installed as well. I loved it when the ceiling wasn't completed yet because opened ceilings made installing the cable much easier since there was no need to remove ceiling tiles.

Phase two would occur once the building was completed. That is when we would install the phone system, outlets and train the users. Training the administrator on how to program the system would often require a third visit.

The most effective and cost-efficient way to install a phone system requires utilizing the list of tasks prioritized by phases, stages, and levels of importance. Without a step-by-step guide for installing phone systems, our company would have struggled to survive.

As noted in **The Foundation Principle**, Nehemiah always consulted God first. In doing so, he recognized that God was priority number one. After that, we see him prioritizing his building efforts. After seeking God, He obtained permission to build. Next, he surveyed the land to ascertain the needs. He then scouted and recruited volunteers. Only then do we see the actual building project get underway. Upon completion, Nehemiah resigned as the general contractor and focused his efforts on full-time governing. He embraced our next principle: **The Prioritization Principle**.

King Solomon spelled out the prioritization principle in Proverb 24:27.

[Put first things first.] Prepare your work outside and get it ready for yourself in the field; and afterward build your house and establish a home.

(AMP, emphasis added)

In his wisdom, Solomon recognized the godly wisdom of properly prioritizing tasks. He understood that to fulfill a vision successfully, one must organize tasks and rank them by importance. When we prioritize, we create and build a solid foundation for our vision to withstand the test of time. I alluded to this principle in **The Foundation Principle** during the discourse about how God created structure. God established priority in the creation process as follows:

1. He hovered over the face of the deep.
2. He created light to bring exposure and set limits for darkness.
3. He created the sky and land to establish boundaries for water.

While we serve a God who can do whatever He wants in any manner that He chooses, I believe he used this principle to set an example for us to prioritize. If I tried to create a prototype of the earth by using a sky and land as boundaries for water in the dark, I honestly believe I'd create a big hot spicy mess instead. Our omnipotent God could, but that doesn't mean we should. Instead, what we can do is use His framework when birthing out our God-given assignment. Here's an example:

1. We begin by hovering over the face of our dreams to determine:
   a. Resources with which we currently have to work.
   b. Obstacles hindering productivity.

    c.   Resources we must obtain to complete the project.

2. We can continue by bringing exposure to the problem that our assignment will address by.

    a.   Alerting necessary authorities by applying for permits and licenses, as required.

    b.   Recruiting people to assist in carrying out the essential tasks.

3. We can create well-thought-out policies, procedures, and protocols to establish team boundaries by:.

    a.   Create job descriptions and task deadlines, for example.

    b.   If necessary, consider including codes of conduct or codes of ethics.

First Things First

Before we launch out into the "Prioritizational Deep," it is advantageous first to reiterate what we discussed in *The Foundation Principle*. Jesus provides clear and concise instructions that also lay the foundation for *The Prioritization Principle*. If we make God our top priority, God will guide us in setting all our other priorities. He specifically said:

> **But seek ye first the kingdom of God, and his righteousness; and all these things shall be added unto you.**
>
> **(Matthew 6:33)**

If we follow this prescription, we will effectively allow God to prioritize our lives. Let's briefly review these basics.

Priority #1 in Matthew 6:33 is to seek the Kingdom of God, which scripture defines as "righteousness, peace, and joy *in* the Holy Ghost."[60] To do this, we must tap into our spirit to practice walking in the Spirit. Ergo, we will walk in right standing with God, causing peace and joy to stalk and overtake us like a predator would his prey.

Priority #2 is to seek God's righteousness. Scripture describes the righteousness of us mere humans as "filthy rags"[61] or, in today's terms, a woman's soiled sanitary napkin. But He, being a righteous and just God, embodies righteousness in His essence. Thus, it would behoove us to humble ourselves and continually seek after His righteousness.

Walking in God's righteousness develops and preserves our integrity. If we adhere to these two priorities first, God has promised that "all these things" shall be added unto us. And His promises are guarantees that you can take straight to the bank.

So, what are "all these things"? "All these things" denotes anything necessary to fulfill God's purpose. "All these things" is associated with the desires of your heart, *provided* you delight yourself in Him.[62] "All these things" equates to any area of lack. God promised to "add" in every area of lack in our lives *if* we seek the Kingdom of God and His righteousness first.

It is not God's will that we should be "anxious about anything."[63] We don't have to be anxious because as we seek the Kingdom of God, He will provide us with the instructions for carrying out the task at hand. The instructions could range from specific directions on performing a specialized task to referring us to individuals who can provide us with the blueprint for proceeding. He often places these people in our path to help us discern our next course of action.

I'm not advocating that we just fast and pray our lives away without working. God has already provided us with enough of "these things" to enable us to stay busy even while praying and fasting. If you already know how to build a house, you don't need divine direction to build it. Remember, faith without works is dead. Just listen to what James said:

> **Yea, a man may say, Thou hast faith, and I have works: shew me thy faith without thy works, and I will shew thee my faith by my works.**
>
> **(James 2:18)**

Where To Begin?

Once you have set the first two priorities in order, it is crucial to begin prayerfully establishing a Spirit-led plan of action. Plans help by keeping focus intact while providing a systematic workflow until the assignment is completed.

After the devastating economic effect of Covid-19 worldwide, Global Growth Ministries launched a humanitarian aid program called Helping Hands. The Helping Hands program endeavors to assist people who are struggling economically, especially in countries where very little to no governmental assistance is available.

Unfortunately, the urgency that our first beneficiary faced caused us to jump the gun and begin the relief efforts before the appropriate paperwork, policies, and procedures were in place. We were able to assist, thankfully. Nevertheless, the beneficiary could have achieved the desired outcome sooner, and operations would have run smoother had we solved this crucial part of the puzzle.

The task of establishing protocol, policies, contracts, and other duties may feel overwhelming. Prioritizing these tasks can make for smoother sailing once your endeavor is in full swing. Fortunately, our first client was in a very close relationship with us. Furthermore, God already greenlit the assignment before the client ever even approached us. Sadly, this isn't always the case. I shudder to imagine the outcomes if He hadn't.

What do you do when you receive a mounting pile of tasks required to accomplish your assignment? How do you refrain from giving up in frustration? The answer is in the old proverb: How do you eat an elephant? One bite at a time.[64] Here is a five-step process you can use to slice that elephant up into bite-sized portions.

Step 1: Create a task list.

Brainstorm to create a list of every task you can conceive that is required to launch your project. Don't worry if you don't remember every task. Other tasks will emerge once you start digging in.

Step 2: Categorize tasks

Organize the tasks by creating categories. Group tasks that have common attributes. For example, group all financial tasks together. Administrative tasks may comprise the second group. Technical tasks would have their own category.

Step 3: Break larger tasks up into smaller sub-tasks.

For example, to open a bank account, you may first need to apply for an Employer ID Number. You may also need to open a PO box and create an email address for the business. Knowing each sub-task will assist in completing the larger task.

Step 4: Create step-by-step processes needed to accomplish each task.

In the bank account example, this may not be necessary. However, if you are creating a website yourself, you must learn each step of that process. For example, before designing the website, you must secure a domain and a hosting provider. Next, you must choose a platform. Then, you must pick a theme unless you want the tedious task of designing the site from scratch. From there, you must configure the website. Only after you have completed these tasks will you be free to add your content.

Step 5: Rank tasks in order of importance.

It may be more important to create policies and procedures than to launch your website. While you may need to multitask, be sure to focus more time on addressing time-sensitive tasks, such as tasks that have legal implications.

Once you have completed these five simple steps, you can now begin adding them to your daily workload, ticking each task off until your project is complete: For small and startup businesses and organizations, task management software such as Asana, Todolist, and Trello are available to help prioritize tasks. Indeed, a simple spreadsheet can also do the trick as well for those who don't have extra funds to start up. And, let's not forget those who aren't computer or tech-savvy. A simple corkboard on a wall and 3x5 cards could do the trick. Regardless of your preferred method of arranging and organizing tasks, the key is to organize your tasks. Once you can see which piece of that elephant to slice, dive right in.

Vision Preservation

When embarking on a new endeavor, vision preservation in one form or another should be high on your priorities list. There is a great danger in not preparing for the future of your God-given assignment. Just because the vision becomes a reality does not mean that it cannot die. You and your assignment are not necessarily one and the same. This knowledge will help you to preserve the life of your mission, regardless of its phase. One of the most effective ways to preserve your vision is to train upcoming leaders.

Mentorship:

If you were to interview most great leaders, you might discover that most, if not all, had a great mentor. Without mentoring upcoming generations, our legacies and visions are subject to death or dismemberment. Moses mentored Joshua. Ruth had Naomi. Timothy had Paul. Elijah mentored Elisha. And let's not forget how Jesus developed his twelve disciples. I would venture to guess that Nehemiah also mentored his brother, Hanani, before assigning him the deputy governor's role.[65]

While it takes extra time and dedication to develop and groom a protégé, the reward of that time and commitment is the ability to offload tasks to someone you can trust. In return for Naomi's mentorship, Ruth (who was younger and most likely much more physically fit) provided food for both of them.[66] While Moses was praying, Joshua was busy serving inside the tent of meeting.[67] The "payment" for Elisha's sacrifice as Elijah's assistant was a double portion of Elijah's spirit.[68]

Consider this scenario: Meet Minister Tom, a rehab therapist. Tom has seen the big picture from the beginning. He saw that God's ultimate purpose for him is to evangelize internationally, helping to rehabilitate people in other countries from spiritual addictions. He recognizes that God ushered him into his destiny through a natural rehabilitation center to prepare him for a global spiritual rehabilitation ministry. Tom is the founder and president of a new Christian drug rehabilitation center. He has been running the center alone for the past year and has successfully rehabilitated twelve people by God's grace. He recently received three new clients.

During the most crucial time of their rehabilitation process, he learned that his mother, who lives in another town, was in a horrific car accident. She needs immediate care. As an only child, he feels responsible for her care. When he arrives at her house to provide what he thought would be temporary care, he learns that her recovery will take several months. What will happen to the three souls he has taken responsibility for in the meantime? How can he move on to his ultimate purpose if he hasn't prepared someone to carry on his current work? These are the types of questions that one must evaluate to ensure vision fulfillment.

Replacement Therapy:

Have you ever experienced a missed opportunity and wished that you would have seized on that opportunity? For example, has something like this ever happened to you? A commercial advertising something you've longed for comes on. You see the words, "ACT NOW WHILE SUPPLIES LAST," fill the screen, but you decide to wait for a better offer. Only a better offer never comes because someone else replaced you as the final buyer while you procrastinated. Losing that product might hurt, but a missed job opportunity would most likely hurt far worse. I'll share a perfect example of the heartbreak of a missed opportunity in *Genie In A Bottle*.

There are a host of reasons for missed opportunities. As those opportunities vanish before our eyes, we often can't help but wonder, "who bought that last gadget," or "who got the job I applied for." Thoughts of how we managed to get replaced begin to bombard our minds, often disrupting our peace.

Sometimes, when people enter positions of power, their focus changes from seeking God for instruction to protecting self-perceived territories. Conversely, some people in powerful positions may feel threatened because they assume that others are attempting to "steal" their title. Meanwhile, they fail to realize that the position is by divine appointment.

God replaces people in leadership positions for varied reasons. Some reasons may have to do with timing. Others could be due to lack of development, to name a few. Yet, there are two motivations that I find quite striking. Either God wants to promote you for a job well done, or He wants to replace you because you were caught with your works undone.[69] Suppose you are not doing God's assignment the way He wants you to do it. In such cases, either your level of success will eventually diminish, or God will step in and replace you with someone willing to do the job more efficiently. I call this "phenomenon" replacement therapy.

In South Africa, I started a ministry called the Prophetic Ministry of the Arts (PMA). We primarily ministered by adding praise dance and mime to church services. We also conducted outreach. While the ministry consisted of members from all age groups, most members were youth or young adults. Even though they all loved to minister, few of them appreciated the amount of time and physical exertion required (older adults included) to minister in excellence.

During devotion, I would often share a story I heard on TV years prior. I didn't know the pastor sharing the story, but his story had a lifelong impact on my life. For the sake of this story, we will call the pastor "John." The story goes something like this:

Pastor John explained that God had given him a vision of a church building. The vision was so clear and detailed that he hired an architect to draw up blueprints. He knew in his spirit that God was leading him from business into ministry. For the next six months, John proceeded to build the church God showed him. It turned out to be the most challenging time of his life, fraught with trials and tribulations. There were times he wanted to throw in the towel, but he persevered until the church opened. John was stunned at the number of people who came to the opening service. He was even more shocked at the scores of people who gave their lives to Christ during the altar call. Every Sunday thereafter for the next six months was precisely like that.

Six months later, a gentleman who attended faithfully every Sunday approached John, asking if he could have a moment of his time. John recognized this man. He faithfully attended the services and was a generous giver during offerings. John observed him weeping every Sunday during the altar call but sensed that they were not tears of joy. He felt that this man was grieved and always wondered why.

John escorted the gentleman to his office. The gentleman – we will call him Carlisle – began to explain the reason for the visit. He shared that ten years earlier, God had given him a vision to build a church. The vision was so vivid and detailed that Carlisle decided to have blueprints drawn up immediately. He then plunged into the job of building the church. Unfortunately, however, Carlisle experienced so many hardships and misfortunes that he ultimately abandoned the assignment and returned to his previous position in the business sector.

After sharing this experience with Pastor John, Carlisle asked if he could show the pastor something. He then proceeded to pull out a set of blueprints he had brought with him. John was flummoxed when he saw the exact blueprints to that very church. John then told the TV viewers, "I wasn't God's first choice." God replaced Carlisle with John because Carlisle could not endure everything it would take to fulfill the vision. Knowing that God had replaced him, Carlisle constantly wept during the altar calls.[70]

I would always conclude the story by telling the PMA members that "you too can be replaced." Sure enough, replacement would often come, and I consistently felt as if it was therapeutic for me when it did. God **always** had a ram in the bush[71] to replace that rebellious knucklehead who would leave kicking and screaming or the student leaving for university. I'm sure it is also therapeutic for God to replace leaders to either bring new life back into a ministry or elevate the "replaced."

Let's not forget how God replaced Moses. God mandated that Moses lead the Israelites into the Promised land. In the books of Exodus and Numbers, we learn that even though Moses was raised as Egyptian royalty, he had a passion for his people, the Hebrews. His passion would cause him to flee into exile for 40 years after murdering an Egyptian for abusing a Hebrew.

God re-ignited his passion when He called Moses to return to Egypt with a mandate to deliver the Israelites from Egyptian oppression. God used Moses to demonstrate various signs and wonders both in Egypt and in the wilderness. Yet, because Moses did not correctly carry out God's instruction in one instance, he forfeited his right to lead the Israelites into and enjoy a prosperous life in the Promised Land.

I always honored Moses for his conduct *after* he received the "sentence" that God handed down. He had to tote the children of Israel around in the wilderness for approximately 38 years after learning that he wouldn't get the privilege of bringing them to Canaan.[72] Just think: Moses knew that God was replacing him. Equally, he understood that God's will was more important than his passion, so what did he do? He developed his replacement so that God's will could continue in the lives of the Israelites. Now *that's* a true leader for you! As painful as it was, he embraced his sentence and empowered his replacement.

The concept of replacement therapy is a difficult lesson for many people to digest. We often hear the expression, "delayed doesn't mean denied," within many Christian circles. That's absolutely true … sometimes. In fact, there are also times where complacency, procrastination, failure to prioritize, or lack of preparation will cause the ship of opportunity to sail right past you. Therefore, when leading any venture, you must always be sensitive to your expiration dates and those who report to you. Adding mentorship to your program and becoming receptive to replacement therapy will lay a solid foundation for vision fulfillment and aid in conquering at least one item in your priorities list.

Key Takeaways:

→ Prioritizing tasks helps to focus attention on the most critical tasks. It also helps combat feelings of being overwhelmed.

→ *The Prioritization principle* dictates that one must build organization into plans to guarantee the most effective execution. Otherwise, improperly prioritized tasks could either delay or halt project execution.

→ Raising mentors ensures that your legacy continues, thus preserving your God-given assignment

Reflections:

→ Consider how you currently prioritize your tasks. What methods can you employ to enhance the way you currently prioritize them?

→ What strategies have (or will) you implement to preserve your vision?

→ What can you do to ensure that God does not replace you after you've agreed to accept the mission that He has assigned you?

Prayer:

Gracious Jesus, thank You for teaching me the importance of seeking Your kingdom and righteousness. Please grace me to hunger after Your righteousness as the deer pants after water. Help me demonstrate Your righteousness by fulfilling the vision you gave me according to Your divine instructions. Please teach me how to list my priorities and operate in the spirit of Excellence that You expect. Lord, please help me to incorporate vision preservation into all my plans and goals. I trust that You can preserve me, so I choose to trust You to preserve my vision. For all these things, I depend entirely on You and thank You in Jesus' matchless name. AMEN!

Chapter 5
THE MODEL PRINCIPLE

For Example, Look at Me

Looking unto Jesus the author and finisher of our faith; who for
the joy that was set before him endured the cross, despising the
shame, and is set down at the right hand of the throne of God.
(Hebrews 12:2)

Then I told them of the hand of my God which was good upon me; as also
the king's words that he had spoken unto me. And they said, Let us rise
up and build. So they strengthened their hands for this good work.
(Nehemiah 2:18)

Have you ever noticed that the bar of difficulty in sports is continuously being raised? I remember watching the 1976 Olympics when Nadia Comăneci set a world gymnastics record by receiving a perfect score of 10.0, which broke the scoreboard. At that time, the scoreboard was not capable of displaying a score above 9.9.

Fast forward 20 years and compare her performance to Dominique Dawes and Shannon Miller during the 1996 Olympics. Comparing their performances to Nadia's, Nadia's routine may appear mediocre at best to most viewers. Fast forward ten more years, and the bar for difficulty was set even higher by Simone Biles. Comăneci set a new standard and raised the bar for Gymnastics through the example she set. Miller and Dawes raised the bar again. Then, Biles' stunning performances caused the bar to skyrocket. Through all of their bar-raising performances, they demonstrated *The Model Principle*.

When most of us hear the word "Model," our minds instantly shift to professional models on the catwalk or pictured in magazines. As they gaze into the camera, they give the readers that "come hither" stare. Their very essence is screaming, "Look At Me!" But a simple shift in viewpoint will direct us to the "model" that means "an example for imitation or emulation."[73]

The Christian's attention should always be on the Model of Models; Jesus. He's the one saying, "Look at Me! Then emulate Me!" In John 14:12, Jesus said,

> **He that believeth on me, the works that I do shall he do also; and greater works than these shall he do.**

Providing the appropriate example sets the stage to carry out your vision more effectively. In other words, if you allow yourself to *be* the example, you will raise the bar for greater success.

The way Nehemiah conducted his affairs provides a brilliant framework for anyone who desires success. He modeled ***The Model Principle*** with the class befitting a king. After obtaining permission from King Artaxerxes to rebuild the city, Nehemiah traveled to Jerusalem and surveyed the land to get a clear picture of the size and scope of the task at hand. He wisely kept his plans and desires quiet while he surveyed the area. It wasn't until he clearly understood the current situation and the job ahead that he began to recruit assistants.[74]

What made his presentation to the recruits so enticing? I'm sure his ability to articulate the details of the current condition was impressive. I can imagine the amazement on their faces as they wondered, *this man just arrived a few days ago. How does he know enough detail to collect the necessary materials to build? He must have done his homework!* Or better yet, *when in the world could he have possibly gathered so much information?* Remember, he conducted his land survey at night. Nehemiah clearly demonstrated a natural propensity for being a role model.

You ARE A Role Model!

I'm stupefied by people in the spotlight today who take their position and status for granted. How many times have you heard a celebrity say, "I'm not trying to be a role model"? And yet fans, young and old, often pattern many aspects of their lives off of their irresponsible, self-centered behavior. They simply don't get it. They are role models whether they like it or not. Regardless of their role, whether good or bad, many people pattern their ideals, attitudes, and behaviors from these public figures.

I once saw a TV program that exposed the influence many musical artists have on today's society. The program revealed that Elvis

Presley was considered lewd during his prime. Networks initially censored his dancing because society at that time viewed his gyrations as vulgar. The program then shifted the focus to today's artists, whose target market is the "teeny-bopper" crowd – those under 13 years of age. The artists performed sexually explicit and exploitative acts to sexually explicit lyrics in concert and on videos. I wonder if those celebrities realize how much blood may rest on their hands.

Observation of children's behavior today reveals that these celebrities' behaviors are producing startling results. One day in the 90s, I remember watching a talk show host interview a lady who dedicated her life to helping sexually abused children. She said she worked with many children who started having oral sex as early as seven and eight years old. Today, it's even worse. There are even reports of preschool children engaging in sexual promiscuity.[75] Many people want to be in the spotlight while rejecting the responsibility that accompanies that spotlight. It is our collective obligation to be role models. Paul told Timothy:

> **Let no man despise thy youth; but *be thou an example* of the believers, in word, in conversation, in charity, in spirit, in faith, in purity.**
>
> **(1 Timothy 4:12, emphasis added)**

Whether intentional or unintentional, the life we live is an example for others, especially new and upcoming leaders. As Christian leaders, we must set a godly example through every aspect of our lives, not only when we are in public view. Consequently, when others look at us, they will be able to see Christ in us, the hope of glory.[76] We will also garner more influence, command increased respect, and receive more support because others will desire to experience the Christ they see in us.

People living in sin characteristically have no problem following others in sin. But the Christian who does not "walk the talk" will typically drive the soul away who desires freedom from sin. Given that Jesus is the most outstanding role model of all time, let us look at a few other exemplary role models.

Elijah:

In Second Kings chapter two, why was Elisha determined not to leave his teacher, Elijah? Elijah conducted himself in such a manner that Elisha craved a double portion of his spirit. Elijah's occupation as a prophet inspired him to stay in tune with God's voice regardless of what man had to say. Thus, the wicked royal family, Ahab, and Jezebel despised him.

Elijah spent much of his time alone, running for his life because of his obedience to God.[77] Yet, Elisha desired to walk in Elijah's shoes.[78] Your obedience to God will attract those who want a closer walk with Jesus to you. Elijah's example triggered Elisha's desire to minister to him.[79] The verb minister means "to give service, care or aid; as to wants or necessities."[80] In other words, to minister is "to serve" ... not "to be served." It was Elisha's pleasure to serve the one who set the best example for him.

Moses:

Now consider Moses' conduct in front of his young apprentice, Joshua. Moses conducted himself such that the Bible described him as the meekest man on earth, which is not to say that he was perfect. He was indeed human. His human imperfection kept him from entering the Promised Land. Yet, the Bible says, "God spoke to Moses face to face, as a man speaks to his friend." The God who declared that no man has seen His face and lived esteemed Moses' character high enough to at least vocally speak to him face to face.

Moses didn't physically see God's face during his conversations, but what an honor to have such intimacy with God![81] Can you imagine His eyes intently staring into yours while you hear Him whispering "sweet somethings" into your spirit?

Because of Moses' "righteous indignation" towards the Children of Israel's rebellion, when God told him to speak to a rock so it would produce water, he hit the rock instead. His disobedience caused him to forfeit his right to enter the Promised Land.

Ask yourself: Would you throw up your hands and give up on your years-long assignment after learning that you wouldn't achieve your reward? For most of us, the chances are that we would. But, not Moses! His persistence never wavered. He pulled up his big boy pants and took the time and energy to train Joshua, providing him with the blueprint for leading God's people into the Promised Land.[82]

Moses demonstrated great leadership by continuing to lead even after learning that he couldn't enter the Promised Land he craved for decades. Moreover, he knew how to take accountability like a great leader. Had Moses not set such an example before Joshua, Jericho's walls may have never come down.[83] Likewise, if Moses hadn't developed Joshua, the children of Israel might not have made the trek to Jericho.

Nehemiah:

Finally, let's make an overall observation of the star of this show, Nehemiah. When we examine the project he was responsible for, we see him setting an example for everyone who worked with and for him. He sought the Lord before acting upon the vision God gave him. He went to Jerusalem prepared with a plan and surveyed the area to conduct a needs assessment. Nehemiah knew the importance of staying in his lane. He sought God for the wisdom to fight his enemies and organized his subordinates accordingly. What's more, I doubt he ever took a management, business, or leadership course. Now that's what I call an example to follow! [84]

Triple Filter Test

A thought-provoking story is floating around the internet about Socrates responding to someone who wanted to share information with him about his friend. While the source cannot be confirmed, the message is quite impactful and illustrates what a model looks like.

In ancient Greece (469 – 399 BC), Socrates was widely lauded for his wisdom. One day an acquaintance ran up to him and asked, "Socrates, do you know what I just heard about Diogenes?"

"Hold on a minute," Socrates replied. "Before telling me anything, I'd like you to pass a little test. It's called the Triple Filter Test.

"Triple filter?"

"That's right," Socrates continued, "Before you talk to me about Diogenes, let's take a moment to filter what you're going to say. The first filter is Truth. Have you made absolutely sure that what you are about to tell me is true?"

"No," the man said, "actually, I just heard about it."

"All right," said Socrates. "So, you don't really know if it's true or not. Now let's try the second filter, the filter of Goodness. Is what you are about to tell me about Diogenes something good?"

"No, on the contrary..."

"So," Socrates continued, "You want to tell me something bad about him, but you're not certain it's true. You may still pass the test, though, because there's one filter left: the filter of Usefulness. Is what you want to tell me about Diogenes going to be useful to me?"

"No, not really."

"Well," concluded Socrates, "if what you want to tell me is neither true nor good nor even useful, why tell it to me at all?"[85]

Assuming this account is valid, Socrates's attitude sets him apart as a great philosopher held in high esteem. Socrates walked by example by not allowing himself to become a human garbage can and defending his friend by not allowing an outsider to slander his name. When we protect our friends and loved ones in this manner, we won't allow outsiders to influence us by people who spread their negative opinions. Furthermore, if we have used discernment when selecting teammates, we shouldn't be easily influenced by mindless gossip. Since discernment is vital for selecting God's choice in colleagues, I'll discuss it at great length later.

We have many role models before us, both Biblical and present day, but what example are we setting for people in our charge? We must learn to consider the effect we have on those who look up to us through patterning our behaviors and attitudes after our supreme example, Jesus. Letting this mind be in us, which was also in Christ Jesus, will guarantee that we set a defined standard for others to follow. [86]

Key Takeaways:

→ As a leader, you must remain cognizant of the fact that you are a role model. Thus, emulating Jesus, the Great Role Model, will ensure that your followers see a Godly leader.

→ Many great leaders in the Bible demonstrate how to be role models through a lifestyle of integrity. Integrity is crucial for setting an example.

→ Truth, goodness, and usefulness are the keystone ingredients for Godly examples.

Reflections:

→ Think back over the last 60 days. Consider what type of example you've set. Could you have set a better example? If so, how?

→ Name an instance in your life where you failed the triple filter test. How will you prevent failing it again?

→ Think of three measures that you can take to set a great (or greater) example for your (potential) followers.

Prayer:

Dear King Jesus, thank You for being the ultimate Role Model. Thank You for showing me how a godly role model behaves. Thank You for opening my eyes and showing me how I can walk in integrity, thereby becoming a positive influence to others. Please teach me to reflect Your light, both in public and in private. Show me when my behavior is unbecoming and give me the grace to correct it in Your precious, holy name. AMEN!

Chapter 6
THE LOWLY PRINCIPLE

Featuring Humility

But he giveth more grace. Wherefore he saith, God resisteth
the proud, but giveth grace unto the humble.
(James 4:6)

Then said I unto them, Ye see the distress that we are in, how Jerusalem
lieth waste, and the gates thereof are burned with fire: come, *and let
us* build up the wall of Jerusalem, that we be no more a reproach.
(Nehemiah 2:17)

Thinking back on life in corporate America, I can recall various mental struggles I endured concerning certain managers. One manager, in particular, Edna English, mentioned that she had no idea how to do my job on many occasions. I didn't think it was fair that she made more than twice my salary even though she did not know my job. However, her leadership capabilities, honesty, and humble spirit caused me to strive towards better productivity. I believe that Edna's humility created open doors for her elevation. She had tapped into **The Lowly Principle**: Humility leads to exaltation.

I also learned humility from a hymn I "learned" as an 18-year-old baby Christian. I would sing this song at the top of my lungs in blissful surrender. I sang, "There's not a friend like the lonely Jesus. No, not one. No, not one." For the life of me, I couldn't figure out why He was so lonely. After all, He *is* seated at God's right hand with the host of heaven bowing at His feet.[87]

Some years later, while reading these words in a hymnal, "There's not a friend like the **Lowly** Jesus," I went slack-jawed. Now that He was lowly, not only did the song make sense to me, but I think I enjoyed praising Him through the song more now that He was no longer lonely.

Today, I can appreciate the song much more for the truth it exposes about my Friend, Jesus. He is so lowly that He allowed himself to be exposed to public shame, to be brutally murdered, and to be buried in a tomb to pay the price for my sins.[88] You can't get much lower than six feet deep, and boy, did His sacrifice pay off. Not only did He rise again, but He also redeemed us from the curse of the law[89] ushering us into this dispensation of grace that we currently enjoy.[90] Today, he is exalted, sitting at my Father's right hand, clothed with glory and power.[91] He is the lowly principle personified!

Now let's examine how Nehemiah demonstrated the lowly principle. In his presentation to the elders and nobles in Jerusalem after conducting a needs assessment, Nehemiah didn't solicit people to do the work for him. He asked his recruits to do the job *with* him. He said, "Let *us* build up the wall." He was not afraid to get his hands dirty. He didn't have to do physically strenuous construction work, nor did he have to place himself in a blue-collar position. After all, he worked in the "White House" of Persia. How many people do you know who would give up the pay and prestige of working directly with a head of state to lay brick?

Nehemiah also displayed humility in his conduct with his employer. Here we have a man called by God to undertake what may be the most significant rebuilding project of his time. God has anointed him and given him the capacity necessary to undertake the project. Yet, Nehemiah does not venture off to accomplish his goal until he receives full permission from the man he serves, King Artaxerxes.[92] While he was privileged to work in the palace among royalty, his role as cupbearer was also that of a humble servant.[93]

Even after Nehemiah accepted the governor's role, he did not mentally elevate himself above his workers. His refusal to enjoy the luxury of the governor's bread and wine was proof that in his eyes, there were no "big I's and little you's." He even refused to collect a salary from the king.[94] Although he received a promotion, Nehemiah's reverence for God prohibited him from esteeming himself above his subordinates.

In today's society, we often do not think of humility as a "good thing." Society has rejected humility because it strips us of our pride or dignity. On the contrary, the source of this thinking is the king of pride himself: satan. The apostle John said the pride of life is not of

God. It is of the world.[95] The spirit of pride caused God's anointed cherub, Lucifer, to fall.[96] He began as an angel, just like the rest of the heavenly hosts of angels. He was heaven's "praise and worship leader." Yet his prideful spirit caused him to elevate himself and desire to become a god – or take over God's job. Thus, God abased him.[97] As a result, God evicted him from His presence. He is now the prince of darkness here on earth.[98] At total enmity to God, satan[99] has no hope for redemption. Therefore, Peter instructed the saints to

Humble yourselves therefore under the mighty hand of God, that he may exalt you in due time:

(1 Peter 5:6)

Why did Peter issue this instruction? Because after Jesus disciplined him in Matthew 16:12, and Paul told the world about how he rebuked him in Galatians 2:1-16, Peter clearly understood this fundamental Biblical lowly principle of abasing and abounding:

And whosoever shall exalt himself shall be abased; and he that shall humble himself shall be exalted

(Matthew 23:12)

Jesus, The Ultimate Example:

Before His ultimate sacrifice, Jesus demonstrated humility by washing the disciples' feet, although He was the Messiah of all.[100] The Israelites wore sandals due to the warm climate in Israel.[101] Can you imagine how dirty – and I would assume crusty – the disciples' feet were during their travels? Washing dirty feet doesn't exactly appear to be fun, glamorous, or rewarding. Most of us would never wash someone else's dirty feet unless absolutely necessary.

Instead of the disciples washing King Jesus' feet, the King washed theirs. In this display, He taught His disciples the importance of humility. By serving his disciples, Jesus teaches us that we are saved to serve. Thus, when God saved us, He commissioned us to humble ourselves by serving others the same way He served His disciples.

As we discussed earlier, Jesus then took that humility, not a step but a giant leap further on the cross. When confronted by the governor about the accusations waged against Him, He never said a mumbling word.[102] He was, among other things, stripped, beaten, spat upon, and crucified.[103] When Peter cut off one of the perpetrator's ears, Jesus healed the perpetrator and scolded Peter for defending Him.[104] He demonstrated how true humility manifests itself by being an example for us and humbling Himself on the cross before sinners.

Just as Jesus, God's only begotten son, God made flesh, humbled Himself before us; we must humble ourselves likewise. Being in a power position does not negate our responsibility to serve. A humble leader isn't above serving guests, scrubbing toilets, or staying behind to clean up after adjourning meetings. Regardless of our area of ministry, it is vital always to remember that no matter how high God exalts us, we must remain humble.

Humility's Glory:

The Bible is laden with examples of the glory that rises out of the ashes of humility. One such example is found in 2 Chronicles 33:1-20. When King Manasseh ascended the throne in Israel, he was the epitome of impiety and wickedness. He embraced idolatry and witchcraft so much that he even conducted human sacrifice. His lifestyle is on record as being worse than pagans. He caused the children of Israel to embrace everything God abhorred. Because of his rebellion, Manasseh became captive to Assyrian bondage.

While in bondage, Manasseh "greatly humbled" himself in prayer and repentance. Through his humility, he ultimately regained his kingdom. Just think: Wouldn't his life have been much easier if he simply followed in the footsteps of his father, Hezekiah – a good king – instead of fulfilling his own fleshly desires? Had it not been for his rebellion, however, we would not see such a great example of **The Lowly Principle** of abasing and abounding acted out.

Another example of humility's glory is found in 2 Kings chapter three. The story begins with the king of Moab revolting against Joram, the king of Israel. Joram and Jehoshaphat (the king of Judah) allied against Moab and agreed that their attack route would be through the desert of Edom. Unfortunately for them, they forgot to consider one important detail: There is no water in the desert. After seven days, their water supply was gone. In desperation, they chose to seek the man of God. Jehoshaphat asked if there was a prophet in the land. One of Joram's officers remembered Elisha, who "poured water on the hands of Elijah."

Everyone knew who Elijah was, but Elisha was still in obscurity. Elisha had recently graduated from his "Prophetic Training Course" under the tutelage of Elijah. As a result, Elisha was only known as Elijah's "water boy," even though he carried a double portion of Elijah's spirit. God used his humble reputation as a water boy to allow his gift to make room for him and bring him before great men.[105]

Regardless of your leadership level, it is imperative to maintain humility irrespective of your post and allow God to promote and exalt you. It is easier to humble yourself than to be lifted in pride and have

God humiliate you. Don't forget the old adage: "The bigger they are, the harder they fall." Proverbs 16:18 echoes this sentiment when it says, "Pride goeth before destruction and a haughty spirit before a fall."

Humility Vs. Meekness

When Pastor Mazibuko came to visit our church in the US, I introduced him to Pastor Badan, the pastor of the church I attended. After the meeting, Pastor Badan – the humblest person I've ever known – said, "He is a very humble man." At the time, I couldn't articulate how I felt, but I never thought of the visiting pastor as humble. So began my quest to determine the difference.

We often use the terms humble and meek interchangeably, but they have very distinct attributes. According to Oxford's English and Spanish Dictionary, humble means "having or showing a modest or low estimate of one's own importance."[106] Conversely, being meek means being "Quiet, gentle, and easily imposed on; submissive."[107] I believe it is much easier to display meekness than it is to show humility.

The Bible describes Moses as the meekest man on earth.[108] Because of his meekness, he readily obeyed God's commands. Yet he displayed pride in his comment when he struck the rock at Meribah in Numbers 20:10 when he said, "must *we* fetch you water out of this rock?" Pride is boastful. His statement revealed that he boasted in himself instead of the God of Glory, presenting himself as the miracle worker.

Moses differed from Paul, who displayed humility when talking about his constant battle with sin in Romans chapter seven. In it, Paul said he didn't understand his actions in verse 15. Paul continued by declaring that nothing good dwelled in him in verse 18. He then called himself wretched in verse 24. Finally, after revealing all of his flaws, Paul humbled himself in public worship by glorifying the Lord. He also showed his humility when he shared his credentials with the Philippian church.

> **"If anyone else thinks he may have confidence in the flesh, I more: circumcised the eighth day, of the stock of Israel, of the tribe of Benjamin, a Hebrew of the Hebrews; concerning the law, a Pharisee; concerning zeal, persecuting the church; concerning the righteousness which is in the law, blameless. But what things were gain to me, these I have counted loss for Christ."**
>
> **(Philippians 3:4-6)**

Paul then goes on to discount all his credentials as rubbish[109] to gain Christ. Unfortunately, humility like this is challenging to find in society. Still, God has blessed me to witness humility on display through Pastor Badan. There are a few occasions where I've heard him reveal what he referred to as an embarrassing moment or a character flaw. On one occasion, Pastor Badan shared a story about how he thought he was experiencing a heart attack in public, which turned out to be a panic attack.

On another occasion, during a minister's training class, the subject of fear came up. I shared that while I didn't fear death, I *did* fear any pain associated with death. In response, Pastor Badan told me that this was something I needed to overcome. The following Sunday, he all but echoed my words as he shared that he doesn't fear death, but he fears any pain associated with it. While his confession astonished me, his willingness to humble himself publicly once again to echo my fears taught me what true humility looks like.

I would be remiss by not disclosing the humblest man on earth: Jesus Christ. This Man who never even knew sin humbled Himself enough to *become* sin so all humankind can be set free from sin's bondage.[110] Who Does That? Apostle Paul had this to say about Him in Philippians 2:5-11:

> **"Let this mind be in you, which was also in Christ Jesus: Who, being in the form of God, thought it not robbery to be equal with God: But made himself of no reputation, and took upon him the form of a servant, and was made in the likeness of men: And being found in fashion as a man, he humbled himself, and became obedient unto death, even the death of the cross. Wherefore God also hath highly exalted him, and given him a name which is above every name: That at the name of Jesus every knee should bow, of things in heaven, and things in earth, and things under the earth; And that every tongue should confess that Jesus Christ is Lord, to the glory of God the Father."**

Now that's what I call humility on steroids! Pastor Mazibuko, on the other hand, was a meek man. A Zulu man steeped in South African culture, he was raised to be meek.

On one of my flights from South Africa, the gentleman I sat next to told me that South African blacks were the proudest people he had ever known. Needless to say, I had to reconcile his opinion with how Pastor Badan perceived Pastor Mazibuko. While the host pastor was indeed meek due to his Zulu upbringing, he was also quite proud.

I observed this contrast in many black South Africans during my stay. Except for one close friend, I doubt I can count on one hand the number of genuinely humble South Africans I know. Most, however, are rather meek. It's a cultural thing.

One telltale sign of pride masquerading as humility is in the question, "What will people say?" A humble person is much less concerned with what people say than what God thinks. How many times have you found yourself asking what people would think or say about your actions? That simple question can determine if your action or behavior is motivated by pride.

Now that we have distinguished between humility and meekness, we're ready to take the plunge into *The Servant Principle*.

Key Takeaways:

→ A humble leader has no problem working alongside – or even for subordinates.

→ Creating an atmosphere of "Big I's and Little U's" is a dangerous element in a project that can threaten its effectiveness

→ There is a distinct difference between being meek and being humble. Meekness is solely grounded in service, while humility doesn't shy away from perceived public shame.

Reflections:

→ Reflect on a situation where pride became a hindrance in your life. Describe the problem and the steps you took to correct the issue (if any).

→ How can you actively demonstrate true humility while maintaining the respect of your subordinates?

→ Can you recall a time that you became concerned about what people would think concerning something you felt God wanted you to do? If so, how did you reconcile what people thought with what God said?

Prayer:

Lord Jesus, once again, You've demonstrated the type of spirit You long for Your bride to embrace. Not only are You the perfect role model, but You, the King of kings, humbled Yourself to the level of a lowly servant. You served my sin up on a silver platter to my Father so that I won't have to. Thank You for loving me enough to make such a sacrifice. Thank You for humbling yourself by taking on my sins.

Thank You for showing me how a humble leader looks. Grant me the grace to live in Your shadow. Forgive me for times that I esteemed people's thoughts higher than your instructions. Reveal when I am becoming boastful or lifted in pride so that I can humble myself under Your mighty hand. In Jesus' name, this I pray. AMEN!

Chapter 7

THE SERVANT PRINCIPLE

Genie In a Bottle

<hr/>

For though I am free from all, I have made myself a
servant to all, that I might win more of them.
(1 Corinthians 9:19, ESV)

And said unto the king, Let the king live for ever ...
(Nehemiah 2:3)

Remember the old fable of the genie in a bottle? The bottle's proud recipient gently rubs the bottle and out pops a genie, ready to serve his master with three wishes. "Your wish is my command," would be the genie's initial greeting. The fantasy was so popular that its concept made its way into homes across America through the sitcom "I Dream Of Jeannie" in the 60s.[111]

The sitcom differed from the original fairytale in that Jeannie was a permanent fixture in the life of her master. While Jeannie possessed all the power, she was always subject to the "master" who had no power whatsoever. Though most viewers would have loved to be in the master's place, few realized who was really in control; the servant, and the star of our next principle, *The Servant Principle*.

While "I Dream of Jeannie" was a fairytale, *The Servant Principle* upholds its implication of servanthood. Ironically, it also glorifies servanthood to a degree. *The Servant Principle* simply states that God elevates those of low esteem. I once heard James Robison echo this principle on his TV show, "Life Today." He said, "Servant-hood is the key to significance."[112] It is beneficial for people in authority to walk in humility and adopt a spirit of service.

Nehemiah, a governor and general contractor, seemed to understand this principle quite well. A general contractor may be qualified to lead a church building project. Likewise, a governor may be competent to rule over a territory. But neither of these experiences qualifies a person to oversee a congregation.

Understanding his place, when Nehemiah finished his construction project, he had no problem stepping out of the limelight. He graciously passed the baton to Ezra to conduct the next item on the agenda: Reading the Law. He readily submitted to Ezra's authority. Nehemiah's conspicuous absence in Ezra's apparent pastoral staff list in Nehemiah chapter eight puts his submission on display.

Contrary to popular belief, service is one of the most vital aspects of leadership. I once heard someone say, "We have enough leadership training classes. What we really need is servant classes." I applauded this comment because of the depth of truth in it. Nevertheless, I'm sure very few people would express an interest in taking a "servant class." A servant class doesn't seem appealing because there is no apparent glory in serving. Few accolades are associated with serving. Yet, one can call Jesus the first Servant Class Instructor. Here's what He had to say about the relationship between leadership and service:

> **But Jesus called them to [Him] and said to them, You know that those who are recognized as governing and are supposed to rule the Gentiles (the nations) lord it over them [ruling with absolute power, holding them in subjection], and their great men exercise authority and dominion over them. But this is not to be so among you; instead, whoever desires to be great among you must be your servant, And whoever wishes to be most important and first in rank among you must be slave of all. For even the Son of Man came not to have service rendered to Him, but to serve, and to give His life as a ransom for (instead of) many.**
>
> **(Mark 10:42-45, AMP)**

In other words, the most effective leader is a servant-leader, which is the kind of leader that Jesus embraces. He demonstrated servant-leadership when He picked up His cross, took on our sins, and endured the shame to give us access to eternal life. Now*THAT'S* Service!

Embedded in human nature is an innate desire to receive glory in one form or another. After all, God created us in His image, and He insists on receiving glory. But the difference between God – the Creator, and us – His creation, is just that. He *is* the creator, thus deserving of all glory. And we, the created, who from the beginning of time allowed sin to pollute our lives, are not worthy of any of God's glory.

Glory Thieves

Few realize the spirit behind the urge to rob God of His glory. Lucifer became a fallen angel and was ejected from heaven because he embraced pride. Pride caused him to desire God's status. He attempted to esteem himself as high as the one who created him.[113] How much sense does this make? No father in his right mind would allow his young son to replace him as a father. Even when the child becomes an adult, the parent typically expects to be honored as the child's giver of life. Lucifer's pride caused him to be converted from friend to foe. I'm sure this is not the kind of conversion the average Joe expects.

People in leadership positions must learn the importance of maintaining a spirit of service. Those who refuse to serve others are typically serving themselves. Consistent self-service is the perfect definition of self-centeredness, which is an ideal prescription for destruction.[114]

Get Wisdom

Leadership circles often contain a body of leaders, e.g., a board of directors, bishop boards, and partnerships. These are leaders with specific roles and responsibilities. In some cases, they are peers. In others, a hierarchy exists. Regardless, everyone in these groups shares the responsibility for a larger group of lay people in some form or other. It is often in these scenarios where we find it necessary to seek sound advice. Whether we are a part of a leadership team or leading in a single capacity, sometimes we must take on a servant's role by submitting to wise counsel. Psalms 1:1 says:

**Blessed is the man that walketh not
in the counsel of the ungodly.**

In leadership, we must submit ourselves to a higher authority, someone we can turn to when we need direction or accountability. Authoritative lines are often clearly drawn when we are in a hierarchical structure. Yet, these lines can be blurred when operating in a peer-to-peer relationship.

Moses, a "solo" leader, took heed to the wise counsel of Jethro, his father-in-law. By submitting to Jethro's advice, he relieved himself of the heavy burden of judging every single case of an entire nation alone. Moses established a subsequent leadership hierarchy by following Jethro's instruction.[115]

Ruth followed Naomi's advice to the letter. Her submission led her right into the hand of her soon-to-be husband, Boaz, a wealthy landowner. King David and King Jesus' paternal lineage includes Ruth's name because she obeyed[116]

Failure to get wisdom has its consequences. One such consequence is manifested in the form of missed opportunities. A friend recently shared about a time when she failed to seek wise counsel many years ago. An opportunity arose for her to work and study in the Netherlands. She applied and waited. In the meantime, another opportunity arose to serve in her local church. Without seeking wise counsel, she seized upon the latter job offer.

Two weeks after accepting the offer to work in her local church, the acceptance letter to study abroad arrived. Instead of seeking wise counsel, she felt honor-bound to her commitment and remained at her church, a place where she has been discontented ever since.

With Covid-19 plaguing society, the effects of her decision haven't escaped her. She knew the opportunity for her to become independent financially awaited her in the Netherlands. Yet, she chose to stay in a place that helped perpetuate the state of poverty in which she now finds herself. That single decision to proceed without first seeking wise counsel is one that she regrets to this day.

The Bible also provides examples of the consequences of failing to heed wise counsel. One can be found in I Kings chapter 12. Rehoboam became the king while he was young. Early in his reign, he subjected his captives to very tough taskmasters. When they begged him to lighten their burden, King Rehoboam first sought the elders for counsel. This is what they advised:

> **If thou wilt be a servant unto this people this day, and wilt serve them, and answer them, and speak good words to them, then they will be thy servants for ever.**
>
> **(1 Kings 12:7)**

These wise elders knew the key to greater productivity. If you serve your servants, they will be forever indebted to you. Unfortunately, however, Rehoboam's inexperience would not allow him to be content with their advice. Thus, he sought counsel from his young, entitled, and inexperienced friends. In their folly, they said:

> **Thus shalt thou speak unto this people that spake unto thee, saying, Thy father made our yoke heavy, but make thou it lighter unto us; thus shalt thou say unto them, My little finger shall be thicker than my father's loins. And now whereas my father did lade you with a heavy yoke, I will add to your yoke: my father hath chastised you with whips, but I will chastise you with scorpions.**
>
> **(1 Kings 12:10-11)**

They underestimated the power of servanthood. The consequence of the king ignoring the elders' wise counsel was an ensuing war and a divided country. Of all the 12 tribes of Israel, God demoted Rehoboam to rulership over only one – Judah.

If you do not know precisely how to proceed in a matter, acknowledge God first. Then allow Him to direct you to wiser or more experienced people if He doesn't answer you directly. Always remember, no matter the capacity or office, we are all saved to serve.

Key Takeaways:

→ Great leaders know how to stay in their lane. Nehemiah knew it was more prudent to pass the baton to Ezra to read the law. Likewise, we must be willing to surrender roles outside our wheelhouse to more suitable partakers to take on those roles.

→ No leader is above wise counsel.

→ The lack of wisdom is a recipe for ruined goals and missed opportunities.

Reflections:

→ Have you ever embarked on a venture that either failed or that you abandoned because you didn't first seek wise counsel? What emotion did the failure or abandonment evoke?

→ As a leader, do you have access to someone you regard as wise to provide you with council?

→ Can you think of a time where you were rewarded for humbling yourself?

Prayer:

Heavenly Father, I praise You for Your example of servanthood through the life and sacrifice of your beloved Son. Please reveal to me times that I failed to seek wise counsel when faced with important decisions. Please give me a spirit to discern when I must seek counsel, not only when leading others but in my life in general. Father, please lead me in the path of righteousness for Your name's sake, and provide me with that "someone" to seek advice from – someone who can hold me accountable to You. I thank You for all these things, in Jesus' name. AMEN!

Chapter 8
THE UNITY PRINCIPLE

Let's Stay Together

━━━━⟨⟡⟩━━━━

Behold, how good and how pleasant it is for
brethren to dwell together in unity!
(Psalm 133:1)

And all the people gathered themselves together as one man into the street
that was before the water gate; and they spake unto Ezra the scribe to bring
the book of the law of Moses, which the LORD had commanded to Israel.
(Nehemiah 8:1)

When I was a kid, there was an old love ballad that I enjoyed by Al Green, called "Let's Stay Together." The song is from the point of view of a man declaring his love for a woman. The chorus says, "Let's stay together, loving you whether times are good or bad, happy or sad." The lyrics remind me of the wedding vows to love, honor and cherish "for better, for worse, for richer, for poorer, in sickness and in health" until death separates the couple.[117] It is from this premise that our next principle is introduced: *The Unity Principle*.

Nehemiah formed a team that shared one goal; build. They may not have seen eye to eye on every minor detail, but everyone in the group stayed on one accord. They had a mind to work. If some focused on non-work-related things, their disjointed mindsets would have hindered their ability to complete their collective task at record speed.

A House Divided

Since my salvation, I have lodged in several places where I've worked with my fair share of ministries. Thus, I've had the fortune to observe the impact of unity – or the lack thereof – on congregations. As a layperson and as a leader, my observations have been consistent.

Unlike the other principles listed in this book, *The Unity Principle* is best described by stating what it is not. Jesus exposed this principle in Matthew 12:25 by painting a picture of life without unity.

> **"Any kingdom that is divided against itself is being brought to desolation and laid waste, and no city or house divided against itself will last or continue to stand (AMP)."**

In *The Foundation Principle*, I discussed how the spirit realm affects the natural realm. Each of our actions is the direct result of a spiritual influence – whether good or bad. Any behavior we exhibit that creates disunity is destructive by nature, even though we may not be cognizant of it.

In Job chapter 1, God held a "court session" with the hosts of heaven. Satan, the accuser of the brethren,"[118] brought charges against Job. During the session, satan accused Job of having the potential to curse God under the right circumstances. He asked permission to cause Job, the defendant, physical and emotional harm. With his wish granted, he launched a full-scale attack, causing the deaths of Job's family, destruction of his property, and subsequent physical attack.

As soon as God granted permission for satan to tempt Job, one gang killed his servants, and another confiscated all of his cattle. Yet another killed more servants and stole his camels. Next, a fire consumed his sheep, and a fierce wind crushed the house where his children were celebrating. As the story continued, Job developed boils throughout his body, and his so-called friends accused him of sinning. They verbally tormented him throughout most of the book.

I'm sure his friends thought they were helping, but they weren't able to discern the influence behind their false accusation. They didn't realize that Job's catastrophic misfortune didn't occur until *after* satan "brought up charges" on Job. Job's predicament was the direct result of spiritual influence. They didn't realize that false accusations are weapons used for character assassination. Moreover, they rarely understand that the godfather of character assassination is the one whose sole purpose is to kill, steal and destroy, according to John 10:10.

Likewise, spiritual influence often stimulates divisive behavioral patterns within leadership. These patterns were birthed in the spirit realm as a form of manipulation and control to induce sabotage. Unfortunately, most leaders who attempt to control or manipulate their followers will often use scripture as a weapon to achieve their goals. While these two spirits influence many behaviors, I'll address a small sample among the most prevalent, which are:

→ Exploitation
→ Favoritism
→ Unhealthy competition

Exploitation:

There are many exploitation tactics that some leaders use to control their followers. For example, elevating someone to a leadership position because they can afford to pay a monthly salary in tithes is a form of exploitation. The elevation is often not Spirit-led but rather a mechanism to keep that follower loyal and the leader's pockets lined. Show me a leader that dismisses people in need to cater to "pocket-liners," and I'll show you an exploitative leader. This type of exploitation divides groups into the "haves and the have nots."

Other leaders exploit members by using fear tactics to maintain faithfulness. Some often do this by prophelying bad things if the follower doesn't comply with the leader's rules or requests.

Favoritism:

Often leaders will give preferential treatment to select members, creating a sense of entitlement among the ranks. While favoritism keeps the entitled members loyal, it usually frays or severs ties between the "inner circle" and the body at large. The byproduct of favoritism is the community-wide spread of the "big I's and little U's" virus. This dynamic can cause those outside the inner circle to feel a sense of rejection.

Unhealthy Competition:

Healthy competition is good; however, when a leader pits one follower against another in the name of competition, no good comes out of it.

Being the target of bullies caused me to hate school, so I wasn't motivated to apply myself. As a result, I mostly brought home B's. One day when I was in high school, my report card contained mostly A's. I couldn't wait to show my mother and make her proud. Instead, she replied, "Cynthia gets A+'s."

My mother comparing my grades with my eldest sister was her feeble attempt to motivate me to do better. Unfortunately, it had the opposite effect. I told her that my name wasn't Cynthia, and I lost interest in applying myself until late in my college years. It was one of a series of incidents that drove a wedge between us that my sister never realized existed.

There are a variety of other behavioral patterns that sow division. As leaders, we must assess the motives behind every action or signal we send. We must consider how our actions or signals can create discord so that we can safeguard team unity.

Unity Maintenance:

Being on one accord is essential in successfully carrying out tasks assigned in the spirit of excellence. In Nehemiah's case, the spirit of unity was so contagious that when they finished the project, the entire community gathered *as one* to hear the word of the Lord and repent.

The word "house" in Matthew 12:25 is indicative of any group. It could represent a family, community, church, or business, for example. If a divided kingdom is guaranteed to fail, how much more would this be the case for any other group? When more than one person comes together to perform a task, remember that you are working as a team, as a group, as one unit. Each person may have a different assignment, skill, ability, and field of expertise. Nonetheless, it is imperative to remember to work cohesively as a team by common consent, especially when appointing committee leaders or choosing people for specific assignments.

The Unity Principle is what Paul sought after when he addressed the Philippian church. He asked that they complete his joy by being on one accord.[119] Paul's message of unity was so important that he begged the Corinthian church to be "perfectly joined together in the same mind."[120]

Paul knew first-hand the dangers of a divided house. After all, his dispute with Barnabas over letting John Mark accompany them on their tour of newly established churches was so fierce that the two parted ways.[121] Yet, even in that instance, Paul and Barnabas stayed on one accord by agreeing to disagree over companion selection and parting ways. Moreover, their mutual desire to check on the welfare of the newly established churches remained intact. The separation did not hinder the vision, mission, and purpose that unified them. Instead, it afforded them the opportunity to visit more cities in a shorter time frame. I suspect the decision was emotionally driven but was also the right decision – a unified decision.

During the discussion of *Vision Preservation*, I mentioned our worship ministry, the PMA. The PMA had its ups and downs. Early on, a few members unsuccessfully attempted to "overthrow" the ministry by starting their own group. We had our periodic verbal knock-down-drag-outs. We faced an excessive number of attacks from people outside of the ministry.

I even recall "firing" the adults' group after being stranded at the church. I depended on public taxis during those days. One evening, only one person showed up for practice, and she was an hour late, which was well after the taxis stopped running. After that incident, my full attention turned to the youth and young adults.

Still, what I adored most about the PMA was how unified we were. Even when we were bickering – myself included – we shared a single purpose: to minister with our whole hearts to the glory of God and to aid in ushering in His presence.

Shortly before my return to the states, PMA members threw a surprise farewell party for me. In typical South African fashion, they each shared how the ministry impacted their lives. I was flabbergasted when they expressed their feelings towards new members while recounting their disdain for the newbies. Some described how jealous they were because they were concerned that the more recent members would rob them of my attention. They jokingly complained about the newbies' behaviors and mannerisms.

I was dumbfounded! We were so unified during ministry and practice that I had no idea how most of them felt about the others before getting to know them personally. I firmly believe that unity was the foundation of the ministry's success.

Leadership Appointments

We should never select people to work with us based on popularity or personal relationship, but rather on divine inspiration. Because of Judas Iscariot's betrayal, the disciples had to select someone to fill the twelfth apostle position so they could begin establishing the church.

The Bible declares that even though 120 people attended the meeting, they *all* "continued with one accord in prayer and supplication." Under God Almighty's leadership, the apostles selected Matthias as the new twelfth apostle via casting lots.[122]

Problems also often arise because of disagreements within a group regarding what a leader presented. These are times to take the issue(s) before the Lord and seek him for revelation regarding the underlying problem so you can root out the cause. Just because you have the vision doesn't mean you have all the answers. Even though your ultimate decision may be final, present others' opinions to God before making the final decision to ensure that you remain in God's will concerning the matter.

Such an incident occurred concerning the daughters of Zelophehad. Their father died in the wilderness while they were single. While Moses was assigning land possession, they approached him, explaining that they should also receive land due to their marital status. When Moses prayed about it, God instructed him to give them land. God then provided him with a new ordinance concerning land issuance in cases of death. Sometime later, family leaders from the Gilead clan of Manasseh met Moses to complain. They argued that if Zelophehad's daughters married outside of their tribe, the Gileadites would forfeit their inheritance to the tribes of the daughters' husbands. Once again, Moses prayed, then shared the words he received straight off the heavenly press! The verdict: the elders were right, so Moses amended the ordinance.[123]

In both instances, Moses listened to the people, took their concerns to God, and amended God's initial commands with His approval. Was God impotent to provide the latter instruction first? I think not. God allows events like these to provide us with teachable moments. In this lesson, we learn that being in leadership does not guarantee that we have all the answers or insight. By being sensitive to our group's concerns, we present a level of flexibility that strengthens unity. Moreover, this flexibility assures people that their opinions are valued and considered.

Let's Get Together

One consistency throughout the Bible is growth and victory among unified people. The common thread is that minds were continually on God, and focus was the same. The underlying tone in every account is, "What is the perfect will of God for the group?"[124] The Bible provides a host of examples of the extraordinary results that people on one accord enjoyed. Three of these instances are:

→ The day of Pentecost
→ The establishment of the Christian church in the form of local assemblies
→ Signs and wonders following the saints

The Day of Pentecost:

The Holy Spirit is a unifier Himself. He entered the scene on the day of Pentecost, fulfilling God's promise to pour out His Spirit upon all flesh. When God fulfilled that promise, where were the disciples? They were sitting in one place with one accord. Visions of tongues like fire appeared and rested upon everyone in the room as they were filled with the Holy Spirit. There were 120 people in attendance, and they were *all* filled. Even Jesus' mother, Mary, was filled with the Holy Spirit and spoke in tongues.

People who heard the disciples speaking their native languages accused them of being crazy or drunk. Peter responded to them by delivering a powerful sermon, which resulted in the church growing by more than 3,000 people on the day of its inception. The disciples then continued *on one accord*.[125]

Churches Established:

In the Book of Acts, we learn that the churches in Asia Minor would have never been established if the disciples hadn't remained of the same mind. The disciples always went out two by two. When issues arose where they were not on one accord, they would set the assignment aside to course-correct, as in the case of Paul and Barnabas.

When your team is not in agreement, you inadvertently open a door for the work that you've begun to be either laden in mediocracy or destroyed. Thus, it would behoove you to stop and, as the disciples did, course correct.

Signs and Wonders following:

When angry mobs would begin to threaten the disciples, they prayed as one and received deliverance. As Paul and Silas praised God with singleness of mind in prison, the power of their anointing caused the place to shake, and an angel opened the prison doors. As believers, we should never run after signs and wonders. Signs and wonders are supposed to follow us. The key to the disciples enjoying corporate miracles and exponential church growth: they were all on one accord.[126]

What do these examples of Godly unification reveal? Extraordinary results. Suppose you want to see your project, ministry, business, class, or church produce exceptional results. In that case, bonding in spirit and tapping into the will of God on one accord is essential.

God's Exception

There is one caveat of being on one accord, which is the purpose for singleness of mind. If the basis for unity is nefarious, God will step in and create division to maintain His purpose.

The Bible illustrates this in the tower of Babel story in Genesis chapter 11. God observed that the people were of one accord, one mind and speech. They desired to build a tower to make a name for ***themselves***. The focus was self, not God. God ascertained that their singular mind and speech could cause the people to do every ungodly thing they set their minds to do. God's solution: confound their language; hence, the birth of multiple nations, tribes, and tongues.

Key Takeaways:

→ Unity births growth and victory. Conversely, division is the prescription of doom.

→ Exploitation, favoritism, and unhealthy competition are three of many forms of manipulation and control that every leader should avoid at all costs.

→ The only time unity isn't acceptable to God is when it is employed against God's will. In those cases, one can expect God to intervene.

Reflections:

→ Have you ever been on the receiving end of exploitation, favoritism, or competition? How did you cope with or conquer these situations?

→ Have you ever found yourself guilty of exploitation, favoritism, or competition? If so, take this time to ask God's forgiveness and course correct.

→ What measures can you employ today to strengthen unity in your group?

Prayer:

Lord God, I come before Your throne of grace, acknowledging from Your Word that a divided group is doomed to fail. Please forgive me for any way I have exploited, shown favoritism, or encouraged unhealthy competition. Lord, I ask for Your mercy. Grace me to embrace and spread a spirit of unity in all my endeavors, in Jesus' name. AMEN!

Chapter 9

THE DISCUSSION PRINCIPLE, PART 1

Can't We All Get Along?

Be ye angry, and sin not: let not the sun go down upon
your wrath: Neither give place to the devil.
(Ephesians 4:26-27)

And I was very angry when I heard their cry and these words.
(Nehemiah 5:6)

Back in the 90s, not long after purchasing my first brand new car, I noticed the police in my rearview mirror on my way home late one evening. I wasn't speeding, but the police continued to drive directly behind me in the middle lane for a while. Very few other cars were on the three-lane road. Thus, I began to feel uneasy driving in the middle lane. I decided to proceed to the right lane to allow him to pass. He immediately turned on his siren, indicating that I must pull over.

I pulled into a gas station and waited for him to approach my vehicle. Within a couple of minutes and for no apparent reason, backup arrived. The police officer came to my car and asked for my license and registration. After verifying my identity, he said he pulled me over because I made an illegal lane change. He said that I hadn't turned on the turn signal before moving into the right lane. Being a person of color and surrounded by cops, needless to say, I felt like I'd become prey to racial profiling.

It was only a few years earlier that police brutally beat Rodney King in Los Angeles. When his words, "Can we all get along?" reverberated across the airwaves at the onset of the 1992 Los Angeles riots, he became the butt of many jokes. Yet, those words have resonated in the hearts of many people since man's fall into sin.

In Genesis chapter three, sin took root in the earth when Adam's transgression caused humankind to fall from grace. Thus, conflict was born. In chapter four, Adam's fall created the atmosphere for Cain and Abel's clash, unleashing a floodgate of sinful acts. Thus, sin created a plethora of circumstances and situations that ignites contention.

Sin in our lives is the root of many issues that hinder us from coming together, thus impeding goal achievement. How can we get along if we never stop long enough to come together and discuss our issues? By applying *The Discussion Principle*. Due to the amount of information that will be covered, I have divided **The Discussion Principle** into two parts:

Part 1: Reveals sources of conflict along with efforts to mitigate conflict.

Part 2: Lays a framework for conflict prevention.

Nehemiah employed **The Discussion Principle** when:

→ He explained his frustration with Jerusalem's conditions to King Artaxerxes. (2:1-8)

→ He responded to Sanballat and Tobiah's jeers. (2:19-20)

→ He gathered the workers to intercede after their enemies devised a plot to hinder their work. (4:7-9)

→ He appointed guards to protect the workers and instructed the workers to work with weapons in hand. (4:16-18)

→ He stopped the rich from oppressing the poor. (5:1-13)

→ He confronted Shemaiah for "prophelying." (6:10-14)

Notably, in Nehemiah chapter 13, while Nehemiah was out of town, Eliashib, the priest who managed the temple, allowed Tobiah, a gentile, to move into a room reserved for tithes and offerings. Where was the conflict, you might ask? Had Nehemiah allowed Tobiah to reside in the chamber, he'd have to provide residence for anyone interested – Jew or Gentile.

More importantly, Eliashib violated protocol, and the violators had to be brought to swift justice. Immediately upon his return, Nehemiah's first response was to right the wrong. He gave Tobiah and his family the "left foot of fellowship,"[127] then had the room cleaned and the rightful property returned. Nehemiah recognized the need to remedy the problem that stemmed from a lack of ethics.

A Question of Ethics

Joshua's great defeat in Joshua chapter seven also illustrates an ethical dilemma. Prior to their battle with Ai, Joshua was not aware that one of the Israelites, Achan, had stolen some things that God explicitly instructed the children of Israel to destroy during the previous war in chapter six. Because of Achan's sin, the Israelites took a severe beat down during their battle against Ai. Achan alone was responsible for 36 deaths.[128]

His lack of integrity and unethical behavior caused the entire nation harm in the form of Israel's first defeat. Achan's sentence was the death penalty for his entire household. It wasn't until Joshua resolved the conflict that the Israelites subsequently conquered Ai in chapter eight.

Organizations collapse all the time. Sometimes poor financial management is the cause. Other times, employee morale hinders growth. Then there are the times when unethical behavior gone unchecked becomes the death of an enterprise.

My sister, Cynthia, once found herself in direct contact with a proverbial Achan. She was a bookkeeper for a small company and struggled for quite some time because the books weren't adding up. In the process of time, Cynthia discovered that one of her colleagues had been embezzling for quite some time. Had the behavior gone unchecked, the potential for two adverse outcomes was in the forecast. My sister could have faced legal jeopardy, and the business could have faced financial failure. Thankfully, keen observation and good communication remedied the situation.

It is imperative to evaluate how to respond if you discover an "Eliashib" or an "Achan" in your midst. What do you do if there is sin, immoral, or unethical behavior in the ranks? In Joshua's case, they tracked Achan down and stoned him and his family to death to atone for his sin and obtain God's mercy. Thankfully, in this dispensation of grace ushered in by Christ's death, burial, resurrection, and ascension, these types of situations are handled a bit differently. Galatians 6:1 tells us:

> **Brethren, if a man be overtaken in a fault, ye which are spiritual, restore such an one in the spirit of meekness; considering thyself, lest thou also be tempted.**

We are often quick to judge people we know in the church who have fallen into sin or are struggling with temptation. Sadly, exhibiting a condemning spirit will often open the door for us to become subject to a greater temptation because of our condemnation. As leaders, scripture requires us to restore that individual in a spirit of meekness whenever possible.

While the law is for the lawless and crimes must be reported, we must refrain from judging or condemning others when necessary. Instead, we must restore. Restoration is often problematic because it is natural to prejudge what we do not know, understand, or have not experienced.

I'm not saying that we should keep transgressors in their positions or continue to permit them to participate in our project. You wouldn't allow a thief to continue to oversee the treasury after you've learned that they stole from the treasury. Still, we are required to forgive and not condemn the thief, especially if they have confessed and repented. Forgiveness in itself is a form of restoration.

Nevertheless, the spirit of self-righteousness, causes us to condemn. We comfort ourselves by esteeming ourselves higher than we should.[129] It is easy to assume that we will never fall into a specific kind of temptation because we haven't fallen into that particular temptation before. A condemning mindset is dangerous, however, because temptation can present itself in a myriad of ways.

For example, it is easy for a person who has never smoked to thumb their nose up at a smoker because that isn't their struggle. Temptation will not knock on that person's door in the form of cigarettes. Instead, temptation will knock on the door of their weakness. So, if you aren't a smoker, but you struggle with lust, guess what temptation you are inviting by condemning someone else for failure to overcome their weakness? You've guessed right, my friend! Your individual weakness.

Escalation Procedures

Matthew chapter 18 addresses how we must handle those who are not just overtaken by a fault but rather live in blatant sin.

> *Moreover if your brother sins against you, go and tell him his fault between you and him alone. If he hears you, you have gained your brother. But if he will not hear, take with you one or two more, that 'by the mouth of two or three witnesses every word may be established.' And if he refuses to hear them, tell it to the church. But if he refuses even to hear the church, let him be to you like a heathen and a tax collector.*
>
> **(Matthew 18:15-17, NKJV)**

This passage provides us with a straightforward protocol for addressing misconduct. As we can see, Jesus lets us know that we must begin by approaching the individual on a one-on-one basis. Then, if the offender still doesn't receive you, move on to the second escalation level; bring the offender before one or two witnesses. Finally, if the person is still content in sin, you must proceed to the highest level of escalation – exposure.

Exposure may appear to be a harsh solution to many people, but it is necessary for project restoration. Moreover, it allows the offender to "destroy his corrupt nature so that his spiritual nature may be saved."[130] Note that at the end of the day, however, one must expose the truth. Hopefully, if no other consequences arise, the exposure can be used to save the transgressing believer's "soul from death and bring about the forgiveness of many sins."[131] Thus, while the transgressor may feel humiliated or ashamed, this might be the very situation that triggers deliverance or salvation.

The Inquisition

When I worked in the telecommunications industry, I knew that many people I worked with struggled with my strong personality. Therefore, I often assured them that they could feel free to discuss anything with me if they ever had a problem with me.

One day, one of our supervisors created an atmosphere for what felt like a recipe for an inquisition during a department meeting. "If anyone has a problem with a peer and feels too uncomfortable to confront the person, feel free to let me know anonymously," she said. "I will make sure to correct the 'problem' individual."

Feeling as if I would soon become the accused, alarms blared in my heart so intensely that I couldn't hold my peace. I responded by telling our supervisor that implementing that procedure would result in witch-hunts. "No court in this country would convict, let alone try a case against an accused party without bringing the accused before his or her accuser," I said.

Ironically, everyone in attendance responded by nodding their heads in agreement and saying things like, "Hmmm, that's true," or "good point." Finally, after much discussion, she relented, and things went back to business as usual. After all, as far as I knew, none of us were witches (I hope). Nonetheless, I sure felt hunted.

Blind accusations have wounded scores of individuals both inside and outside the church walls. Therefore, we must seek God for divine counsel before taking action. I would never want the blood of someone else on my hands simply because of a "gut feeling" or my response to hearsay. These are fragile matters that we must handle with extreme care and through the Holy Spirit's leading.

A more common occurrence of conflict typically arises from opposing opinions or personality clashes. As discussed in *Let's Stay Together*, a major conflict occurred when Paul and Barnabas were preparing to visit their established churches. Barnabas wanted to take John Mark along, but Paul vehemently opposed Barnabas's decision.[132] Many scholars believe Paul did not wish to bring John Mark along because of his lack of follow-through. He had already gone AWOL on a previous mission.[133] In this instance, the only resolution was to abandon their mission to travel together.

In Paul's epistles, we subsequently learn that he developed a great respect for John Mark.[134] Some scholars believe that Paul later regretted his stubbornness in their dispute and apologized for his behavior concerning the matter.[135] Good, clear communication is a vital key to resolving these types of issues.

Key Takeaways:

→ Demonstrating or tolerating unethical behavior invites corruption, which damages the reputation and the future of any organization.

→ Restoration is to be preferred to judgment when one is "overtaken in a fault." Exposure is one such restorative measure

→ Sometimes, people unwittingly falsely accuse others based on misinformation. Unfortunately, these unsuspecting accusers usually don't realize the nefarious influence behind their actions.

Reflections:

→ Nehemiah utilized *The Discussion Principle* on several occasions. How many instances can you recall employing *The Discussion Principle*?

→ Have you ever found yourself falsely accusing someone based on misinformation? If so, once you have discovered your error, how did you rectify it? If you didn't correct it, devise a plan to do so.

→ Have you ever found yourself being the target of character assassination? If so, how did you overcome the stigma left behind? Did you forgive those who trespassed against you?

Prayer:

Gracious God and Father, I thank You for this opportunity to acknowledge areas where I have unwittingly been used as a pawn to assassinate the characters of others. I cannot imagine the suffering they've experienced at my hands. Father, please give me a clean heart and renew a right spirit within me. I thank You for forgiving me. Likewise, expose and forgive those who have conspired against me, those who have attempted to destroy my character. Purify my mind so that I can hear Your heart when You gently correct my actions and behaviors. Grace me to maintain integrity in all that I do. Bless me to live a life befitting the ambassador that You have called me to be. I Bless You for Your restorative powers, for restoring me, and for restoring those who have wronged me. Thank You for showing me that forgiveness is one of many attributes of a Father's love, and thank You for loving me, Father. I bless You as I pray in Jesus' Name. AMEN!

Chapter 10

THE DISCUSSION PRINCIPLE, PART 2

The Conference Room

And I told them of the hand of my God that had been upon me for good, and also of the words that the king had spoken to me. And they said, "Let us rise up and build." So they strengthened their hands for the good work.
(Nehemiah 2:18, ASV)

So if when you are offering your gift at the altar you there remember that your brother has any [*grievance*] against you, Leave your gift at the altar and go. First make peace with your brother, and then come back *and* present your gift.
(Matthew 5:23-24, AMP)

Can We Talk?

Words are phenomenal. They contain a force so powerful that they can shape (or reshape) our lives. It was through the spoken word that God created the heavens and the earth. He said, "Let there be," and there was. Likewise, God created the universe by merely verbalizing His thoughts.[136] It was His words that caused Him to call "those things that be not as though they were."[137] That is to say, words don't just have power. Words *are* power. Words contain so much power that they can create life or cause death.[138] Hence, "The wicked are trapped by their foolish words."[139] Therefore, effective communication is vitally important.

What could conceivably be worse than bosses who will not hear the concerns of their workers? Before labor unions existed, there was very little actual communication between management and laborers. Management often conducted themselves more like dictators than managers. Management mistreatment and the neglect of employees who were tired of cries falling on deaf ears created the perfect atmosphere for the birth of labor unions. Labor unions arose from the need to create a dialog between laborers and management.

Nehemiah employed *The Discussion Principle* by demonstrating tremendous communication skills during his days as a city builder. In chapter five of Nehemiah, he took on the role of union leader by listening to the needy residents' grievances. Upon determining the level of unjust activity that had taken place, he went to the bargaining table with the rulers and nobles. It appeared that the unwritten labor contract was due to expire right in the middle of one of the most significant projects ever launched during Israel's captivity. The wall was only half completed.

At the bargaining table, Nehemiah presented his arguments so astutely that "management" – the nobles and rulers – agreed to the terms of his new contract because they had convicted hearts. Here's the power of effective communication: The laborers never asked for a settlement in their grievance. All they needed was someone to stand up for them. When Nehemiah completed his open rebuke, the nobles and rulers agreed to restore what they'd extorted.

To successfully complete the mission set before us, we must thoroughly communicate that mission to everyone involved in assisting us. Nehemiah provided the perfect example by mediating between the people and the rulers to arbitrate issues and implement reforms. Likewise, project leaders should allow time to meet with co-laborers (regardless of hierarchy) to discuss problems that may arise during the assigned mission's execution.

The following section reveals seven rules for effective communication to help leaders prepare for these types of discussions. While these rules may also apply on a personal, one-on-one level, this section focuses primarily on communicating in group settings. With that said, off to the conference room we go!

Communicative Etiquette

Many scriptures guide us in what I would like to refer to as communicative etiquette. The term "communicative etiquette" describes a group of verbal communication rules designed to help us effectively lead in a manner that directs reflection towards God and away from ourselves. While there is a wide array of scripturally backed practices for enhancing communication skills, the following seven rules provide a framework for creating harmony and synergy in any work environment. I have used slogans to make them easier to remember. They include:

1. Yea Yea, Nay, Nay
2. Think Before You Speak
3. Hurry Up and Hush Up
4. Mark My Words
5. Let Grace Abound
6. Confirm, Confirm, Confirm
7. Listen Up

Rule #1: Yea, Yea, Nay, Nay.

The first rule is the Yea, Yea, Nay, Nay rule – not to be confused with the "watch me whip, watch me nay, nay" rule. Jesus said,

> **But let your communication be, Yea, yea; Nay, nay: for whatsoever is more than these cometh of evil.**
>
> **(Matthew 5:37)**

Jesus brought this up to address the issue of taking oaths. Nevertheless, He declared that *anything* more than this – your "yes" or "no" – comes from evil. There is nothing wrong with having fun and enjoying ourselves. However, when it is time to come together to accomplish a task, we must not allow our fun to distract our focus on what God would have us do.

More importantly, group meetings are not the place for gossip or backbiting in any setting. Oh, and by the way, if you are prone to gossiping or backbiting, maybe you should consider leaving your leadership role at the altar until you are mature enough to refrain.

Furthermore, the purpose of team meetings is to determine how to enhance God's kingdom. Therefore, during meeting sessions, those assigned to perform tasks should stay focused on those tasks and those tasks only. These are not times to go on tangents or indulge in discussions about things you don't know. During these times, keep your conversation God-guided. Therefore, remember to let your yea be yea, and your nay be nay.

Rule #2: Think Before You Speak.

Look at what Jesus has to say about idle communication.

> **But I say unto you, That every idle word that men shall speak, they shall give account thereof in the day of judgment. For by thy words thou shalt be justified, and by thy words thou shalt be condemned.**
>
> **(Matthew 12:35-36)**

Jesus essentially teaches us the importance of thinking before we speak. Pausing to think before speaking makes complying with the Yea, Yea, Nay, Nay rule easier. Therefore, we must learn to weigh our words.

While all things are lawful, all things are not expedient.[140] What you are thinking may be true, but it may not be necessary or beneficial. For example, if you were to look at me and tell me that I'm big and fat, you might be right. But it doesn't help me at all, especially if I'm already insecure about my weight and height.

We must determine if what we are saying is in line with the Word and will of God. Paul replicated this rule when he cautioned the Ephesians not to let any corrupt communication proceed from their mouths. He encouraged them to speak edifying words so the recipient of those words could receive grace.[141]

Many of us also tend to speak before we think. As a result, statements that we will later regret often spew out from our lips. First Lady Shirley Washington of El Paso once shared a story with me that I found amusing. I don't remember the account or my exact response. I *do* recall that my reaction was funny, though not necessarily appropriate. Fortunately, she wasn't easily offended and had a great sense of humor. As she finished laughing, Lady Washington said, "Sharon, I'm going to pray for you some 'Hush Mouth Grace.'" While I enjoyed our fun and laughter, that statement had a lifelong effect on me.

I distinctly remember the first time I prayed for "hush mouth grace." Within hours of praying this prayer, as I was about to say something that would grieve the Holy Spirit, I heard "Shhhhhhh" from within my spirit. I instantly accepted this newfound grace, and since then, that has become one of my guideposts for prayer. So now, in the spirit of walking in "Hush Mouth Grace," let's continue to our next rule.

Rule #3: Hurry Up and Hush Up.

James admonishes us to,

Be swift to hear, slow to speak, slow to wrath.
(James 1:19)

You should always adhere to this admonition, especially when you are in front of a group of people for whom you are setting an example. Suppose, for instance, that you are standing before an audience. You previously had an encounter with someone who happens to be friends with many of the people in your audience. In that case, "airing your dirty laundry" is inappropriate. Instead, leave your laundry in the laundry room. That is between you and God and has nothing to do with your responsibility to lead the group God has chosen you to oversee.

Before you open your mouth, think. Ask yourself, "Is this something Jesus would say? Will this grieve the Holy Spirit? Will this pass the triple filter test?" If not, then chances are, you shouldn't verbalize it. These are perfect times to ask God to set a guard over your mouth.[142]

Here's one more note regarding being swift to hear and slow to speak: When someone raises an issue in an open forum, it is vital that you hear and understand the point as well as the spirit behind the statement whenever possible. Understanding your teammates' concerns will allow you to rehearse your response in your spirit before God and permit the Holy Spirit to guide your response.[143]

Rule #4: Mark My Words.

The time between vision realization and fulfillment is most often long and complex. As such, in Habakkuk 2:2, God encourages us through the prophet to:

> **...Write the vision, and make it plain upon the tables, that he may run that readeth it.**

This prophetic instruction offers a glimpse into the significance of documentation. Documentation assists by:

→ Preserving plans, ideas, and strategies
→ Providing a blueprint for those who are responsible for carrying out your goals
→ Creating paper trails that protect from fraudulent or deceptive activity

With proper documentation, words can become legal and binding. Hence, it is essential to document everything discussed in meetings. In 1 Corinthians 14:33, Paul says,

For God is not *the author* of confusion, but of peace, as in all churches of the saints.

We should take thorough notes and make sure that everyone hears and agrees with the discussion points so that they may "run that readeth it" before the meeting ends. When permissible, I recommend distributing copies of the meeting notes to all affected parties.

Of course, as the meeting leader, it would be difficult for you to take thorough notes yourself. Therefore, it is wise to delegate this responsibility to an individual present with solid note-taking skills. An alternate option would be to record the meetings for later review. In this manner, you can extract all the information needed to continue to conduct business.

Rule #5: Let Grace Abound.

Salt is a preservative. What comes out of our mouths should help preserve others in Christ. Paul commissioned the Colossians to:

Let your speech be alway with grace, seasoned with salt, that ye may know how ye ought to answer every man.

(Colossians 4:6)

When we are leading people, we must remember to scrutinize what we are saying. We must ascertain whether or not our conversation is edifying. Let's perform my version of the Triple Filter Test. Ask yourself the following three questions.

1. Will what I am about to say edify my audience?
2. Will my audience be encouraged by my words?
3. Will my words draw my audience to Christ?

If you cannot answer "yes" to all three of these questions, abstain from vocalizing that thought. Practicing this rule gives us insight into how to answer everyone.

Rule #6: Confirm, Confirm, Confirm!

At the beginning of this book, I mentioned that God always confirms His word. In fact, the scripture says that He has not "neglected to leave some witnesses of Himself."[144] Hebrews 12:1 tells us that we have a "great cloud of witnesses" surrounding us. Still, Paul gave the church of Corinth the key to mitigating conflict. He said:

"In the mouth of two or three witnesses shall every word be established."

(2 Corinthians 13:1)

The members of your audience *are* your witnesses. Therefore, be sure to confirm that your audience receives the thoughts you are attempting to convey in the context with which they are intended.

Always make sure that everyone agrees on the discussion points. Everyone may not agree on decisions, but everyone should agree with the discussion items raised. In other words, while everyone may not agree on outcomes, everyone should agree on the options presented, and everyone should acknowledge meeting outcomes.

People process what they hear differently, which creates yet another challenge for leaders. Yet, our responsibility is to develop ways to ensure that our colleagues clearly understand what we are expressing. Thus, consider allowing others to share discussion points in their own words when time permits. As a result, you will ensure that your audience understands the idea or thought you are attempting to convey.

Once, before search engines were as effective as they are today, while I had been fasting, I heard the voice of the Lord say, "Arise, slay, and eat." I hadn't been feeling well, and I was trying to sleep. Not realizing that it was the Lord speaking to me, I simply responded, "I don't feel like it now," and proceeded to doze back off when He repeated, "Arise, slay, and eat." This time, I knew it was God, so I arose. Thankfully, the meat was already slain, so I was left with the easy part; cooking and eating it.

I wondered why God had me break my fast this way. At first, I thought He would heal my body because of my obedience to His instruction. Yet, I still didn't feel well when I finished eating, so I asked Him why. He replied, "Search the scriptures."

I already knew of the passage in Acts chapter 10 where God told Peter to arise and eat, so I proceeded to look for that scripture in my electronic Bible. But the only scripture it would point to was in 1 Kings 19. I did not want that scripture. I wanted what I wanted! So, I pulled out my Thompson-Chain Reference Bible and began to diligently search until I found the passage I knew in Acts, which seemed to take forever. I understood what was happening in the text, but I had no idea what it had to do with me.

I then remembered that Psalms 1:2 tells us that the blessed man meditates on God's law both day and night, so I began to meditate diligently on the passage in Acts. I racked my brain for hours seeking an understanding and getting nowhere. Finally, some days later, I shared this experience with Pastor Mazibuko, who responded, "God is trying to get your attention. When He repeats himself, He is trying to alert you." He then proceeded to explain, "Just like God told Elijah twice to arise and eat because this journey is too great for him, He is telling you the same thing." And of all places, can you guess where I found that scripture? That's right! In 1 Kings 19!

At the time, I was preparing for my first missionary trip to South Africa, and I needed to build my physical strength. God told me in two different ways. He first spoke to me directly. He then referred me straight to the scripture that applied to me in my electronic Bible. Still, my stubbornness kept me from realizing that God was using my electronic Bible's search function to tell me what scripture to read, so I ignored Him in an effort to understand Him. Psychologists may explain my faux pas by suggesting I fell prey to the *Einstellung Effect* (blocked thoughts due to preceding training).[145] I call it the "Duh" factor.

I did not process what God was telling me because of how I chose to interpret what He was telling me. Thanks to God's grace, He sent me another human to articulate what He'd been trying to say directly to me all along.

Just as God communicates in various ways, we as humans do as well. Likewise, as leaders, we must become acquainted with the varied ways people communicate and how they process what we are saying. In doing so, we can more effectively articulate our ideas, needs, and issues.

Rule #7: Listen Up!

In Judges chapter 12, the Ephraimites started a war with the Gileadites. The Gileadites defeated the Ephraimites and took over the parts of the Jordan River that crossed into Ephraim. When an Ephraimite attempted to cross the river, the Gileadite would ask if they were from Ephraim. To catch him in a lie, the Gileadite would tell them to say "Shibboleth" because he knew that Ephraimites couldn't pronounce it correctly. When the Ephraimite would respond with, "Sibboleth," he would be caught and killed. The Gileadites learned to listen well enough to distinguish between cultural dialects.

I believe that all leaders should consider taking time to improve their listening skills. Furthermore, leaders who intend to minister in other cultures should either learn enough about the local dialect to communicate effectively or retain an excellent interpreter to ensure that your message doesn't get diluted or misinterpreted.

A Setswana-speaking interpreter once told me that Setswana is a straightforward language because it doesn't contain all the homonyms and synonyms contained in English. There is also very little slang used in Setswana. As a result, there are not that many different ways to say the same thing. After learning this, I began to observe the locals more closely as they communicated. From my perspective, the level of miscommunication in South Africa did not appear to exist on the scale we often see here in America.

Sometimes, when communicating, we either don't hear the inquiry in its entirety or realize that our response is not the actual answer. These instances can lead to confusion, frustration, or inappropriate actions. I've learned this lesson from being on both ends of this spectrum.

Once, as I was preparing for church, I put on a pair of pantyhose that did not fit properly. When I arrived at church, I ran into a young lady in the hallway. At the end of our short but pleasant conversation, I said, "I need to go to the restroom now because these hose are getting on my last nerve.

"Aunt Sharon," she replied after pausing to wrap her head around my statement. "Do you know what I heard? 'I need to go to the restroom now because these hoes are getting on my last nerve.'"

Before clarifying what I meant, I found myself in a squatting position for a few minutes because my legs became so weak from laughter. Then, choking back the laughter and accompanying tears, I told the young lady about my hose-saga, which rendered her weak with laughter as well. She explained how she had begun interceding for me because she couldn't imagine what the saints could have possibly done to me to cause me to call them hoes.

On another occasion in South Africa, my dear friend, Pastor Naido Selokela, and I were walking down the street deep in conversation. She ended a statement she made with the words, "Wa bona," which I assumed meant, "do you see" – as in "do you understand." At this point, I was beginning to understand several of the Setswana words and phrases, including this one – or so I thought. I wanted to make sure that my interpretation was correct.

"Wa bona? Does that mean "do you see?" I asked.

"No," she replied.

"What does it mean?" I asked, now becoming quite confused.

She pondered for a moment gazing up to the sky, then slowly said, "Do … you … see."

Needless to say, I was fit to be tied. So, I gave Naido one of those "did I just hear what I thought heard" looks before asking, "Isn't that what I just said?" A chorus of laughter ensued, but to this day, I'll never let her live that one down.

It will be wise to sharpen your listening skills to avoid mishaps like these and more serious ones, of course. Ergo, peace and understanding can replace confusion and frustration.

If we apply these suggestions to our daily communication, we will experience a decline in our level of communication-related frustration. I understand that this takes constant and consistent work on the part of everyone involved. Yet, as leaders, we must continuously be aware of our conversations. While that can be a job in itself, it will prove very rewarding.

Effective communication is the most critical key to success, and the lack thereof is the easiest path to failure. Without effective communication, there can be no relationship. Communication breakdown is one of the highest cited reasons for divorce.[146] Poor communication can divide homes, relationships, countries, and kingdoms.

The observations revealed in **The Discussion Principle** only scratches the surface of communication issues. However, armed with the strategies listed, let us begin implementing these practices and techniques so we can start paving the road to vision fulfillment.

Key Takeaways:

→ Words contain a force so powerful that they can shape (or reshape) our lives. Thus, proper rules for communicative etiquette will improve negotiations and make conflict management simpler.

→ Implementing "communicative etiquette" rules ensures that communication lines are opened, thus minimizing instances of unnecessary conflict.

→ As leaders, we must make it our priority to sharpen our listening skills.

Reflections:

→ Considering the power of your words, are there words you wish you could take back? If you could take them back and replace them, with what words would you replace them?

→ Think back to some of the most significant communication breakdowns that you unintentionally caused. It can be something as simple as a response to something you thought you heard. It can also be something you've conveyed that others misinterpreted. Were you able to rectify the situation(s)? If so, what was the remedy? If not, devise a plan to mend those fences.

→ Thinking of the seven communicative etiquette rules, determine which rule(s) you need to strengthen.

Prayer:

Dear Jesus, I acknowledge You as the Great Communicator. Teach me to communicate as You communicate. Give me the holy boldness to speak what You would have me to speak without fear of reprisals. Teach me hush mouth grace so that I don't grieve Your Spirit or offend others. Give your servant the wisdom to stand as a mediator when needed and the grace to escalate issues when warranted. I thank and praise You for all these things, in Jesus' name, AMEN!

Chapter 11

THE CALENDAR PRINCIPLE

Now is the time

And God said, Let there be lights in the firmament of the heaven to divide the day from the night; and let them be for signs, and for seasons, and for days, and years:
(Genesis 1:14)

And the king said unto me, (the queen also sitting by him,) For how long shall thy journey be? and when wilt thou return? So it pleased the king to send me; and I set him a time ... So I came to Jerusalem, and was there three days.
(Nehemiah 2:6, 11)

n *Seek Ye First*, I mentioned an instance where God redeemed time by granting my petition to have my camcorder delivered before I ministered during a conference. That isn't the only incident where I watched God add His "super" to my natural.

Another incident occurred during a journey home from a cross-country road trip. Several of us were taking turns driving. I was to drive during much of the last leg from Albuquerque to Phoenix. During the tail-end of the journey, we passed Sedona, with 90 minutes of travel left before arriving in Phoenix. As we began driving through the mountains, I noticed the sun starting to set in the west.

My brother, Dwight, once taught me that it takes 8 minutes and 20 seconds for light to travel from the sun to land on earth. Therefore, it takes 8 minutes and 20 seconds after the sun has completely descended below the horizon to get dark.[147]

I don't have the best night vision, so I'm uncomfortable driving in unfamiliar territory at night. So, as the sun slipped behind the horizon, I whispered a prayer asking God to favor me with a Joshua 10:12 miracle – to stop the sun from setting until we arrive at our destination. Then, I quietly declared, "Sun, stand still." For the next 60 miles, I kept an eye on God's "90-minute" sunset.

Once we pulled into the driveway of our destination and exited the vehicle, darkness finally descended. I didn't share my prayer until we were getting out of the car. Then, of course, a chorus of praise ensued.

Unfortunately, these occurrences are a rare exception, not the rule. I once heard the late Archbishop Veron Ash share the story of a woman for whom he had a word from the Lord. He said God had given him a word for her while he was preaching, but when Bishop Ash called for her to come and receive the word, he discovered that she had already left the service.

Others who were at the service later told her that he had a word for her. The next time she saw him, she asked him what the word was. He explained that it was too late. Her season had passed.

God is gracious and often redeems these missed opportunities, but not always. Therefore, it is wise to be cognizant of our timing, responding immediately to the Holy Spirit's prompting.

King Solomon was a man gifted with wisdom that God imparted into him directly. We can find the wisdom that Solomon exuded in his many writings. The Book of Ecclesiastes – purportedly written by him – reveals the intricate details of the measure of his wisdom. Chapter three shows the actual relevance and importance of time and how it relates to God's purpose for us in its definition of *The Calendar Principle*. Verse one says,

> **To every thing there is a season, and a time
> to every purpose under the heaven.**

Nehemiah's timing was purposeful. When he heard about Jerusalem's dilapidated condition, he immediately consecrated himself before God for "certain days."[148] During this period, he sought God for favor with the king. He heard the news during planting season. It was not until three to four months later, during harvest season, that he presented his case to the king to rebuild.[149]

Had Nehemiah gone to the king immediately after praying, the king may well have rejected him. Had he approached the king without allowing God to set the stage for him by causing the king to confront him, again, rejection may have been his portion. But in God's perfect timing, his request was granted.

Once the king permitted him, Nehemiah began the work without hesitation or delay. He knew his season had come. Nehemiah knew when to wait patiently and when to prepare for war. He also knew when to seize on opportunities. He completed his restoration project very quickly because he perceived the importance of God's timing.

Since we did not create time, we find many instances where timing is out of our control, thus seeming to work against us. For example, Solomon notes that there is a time to die. In scripture, we can find many instances where people lived a full life, said their parting blessings, and then died upon completing their purpose. It was their time to die.

Conversely, we can also find cases where life was cut short often because of sin, rebellion, disobedience, unexpected sickness, accidents, and other "untimely" events.

Then there's King Hezekiah's case. The Lord told him in Isaiah 38:1-5 to set his house in order because he was sick "unto death." Yet, God heard his cry and gave him 15 more years because he sought the Lord to save him from death.

But there was an issue. When God told him to get his house in order, he had no sons with whom to pass on the royal baton. In those extra 15 years, Hezekiah had enough time to conceive Manasseh. Remember him? I mentioned him in *The Lowly Principle*. He was by far the worst king in Judah. Some even argue that he was worse than Ahab.

He went as far as slaughtering his sons as a sacrifice to pagan gods. His sins opened the doors for Judah to fall into Babylonian captivity.[150] Yes, he repented, but Judah didn't regain national freedom until Israel became a nation in 1948. As a result, some could argue that Judah's plight resulted from Hezekiah not submitting to God's perfect will to die according to God's perfect timing.

Now, let's fast-forward and consider the timing of current events and their relation to the Covid-19 pandemic. Not long after it arrived in the United States in early 2020, I watched this deadly virus claim the lives of the old and young alike. Unfortunately, as the virus spread like wildfire, the level of disinformation was spreading just as fast, infecting masses of Americans who dismissed the virus as a hoax.

A news program reported about a 30-year-old who died after contracting the virus at a "Covid party." The purpose of Covid parties was to congregate with an infected person deliberately. The Covid victim's last words were, "I think I made a mistake. I thought it was a hoax". He unknowingly took his own life into his hands, and the result was a life cut short. While some may blame this man for his death, others may be tempted to inquire of God concerning His sense of timing.

For example, reflecting on the issue of police killing people of color, some may dare to charge God for allowing them to die before their time. But what gives us this right? God didn't start the racial injustice that's wreaking havoc in the USA. Moreover, we didn't create time, and we certainly didn't create life and death. However, we were all allotted a certain amount of time to fulfill the purpose God created us to achieve. The question then becomes, what have we done to achieve our God-given purpose on this earth thus far?

Why did God create time in the first place? After all, He is an eternal God, dwelling in an eternal heaven. He is God, and He exists where time does not exist, and He certainly doesn't need time for anything. God created time, especially for us, the humans born into a world God foreknew would fall into sin. He created time so we could use it to

→ re-establish our fellowship with Him,

→ discover and fulfill our purpose in Him,

→ and take advantage of the opportunity to spend eternity with Him.

Let's look at a couple of Biblical instances where people wasted time and the resulting consequences. First, there is the parable of ten virgins in the 25th chapter of Matthew. In this parable, five were wise, and five were foolish. All the virgins knew that their bridegroom was to come. None knew when, but they all knew that they should be ready for this exciting event. The five wise virgins prepared. They packed wisely. They knew they would need oil for their lamps, so they made sure to take oil with them.

But the foolish virgins left their oil behind. When the announcement came that the bridegroom was coming, the foolish virgins, who couldn't persuade the wise virgins to share their oil, found themselves on a wild goose chase. I'm sure they ran from shop to shop trying to purchase more oil. By the time they returned, the bridegroom had already entered the party. The five wise virgins were invited to join the party. The door was then closed on the late-coming virgins, with the "bouncers" relaying this ominous message: "I know you not."[151]

How many times have we missed precious opportunities because we failed to prepare for those opportunities? How many times have our season of blessing slipped through our fingers simply because we allowed distraction, complacency, or procrastination to blur our focus? Even in small things, we can miss crucial opportunities if we fail to learn to respect the time God has allotted for us.

That brings us to the parable of the talents Jesus shared in Matthew 25:14-30. In it, a man entrusted three of his servants with talents or "bags of money"[152] before leaving for an extended journey. He instructed them to invest the money to increase the owner's wealth. The employer greatly rewarded the two men who multiplied their money bags by promoting them. He called them "good and faithful servants." This illustration shows us that we must learn to use the time and resources God has given us if we would like Him to entrust us with greater leadership responsibilities.

The parable then describes the third man, who, out of fear of his master, buried his bag of money instead of investing it. The master called him wicked and slothful because he did not invest with his money bags. So, instead of promoting the servant, the employer stripped him of what he had and demoted him.

So often, we allow fear or distractions of current circumstances to blind us from seeing our vision's full potential. We, in turn, fail to invest the time and effort required to bring it to pass.

The man who wasted his investment opportunity was stripped of his responsibilities because he did not wisely use the time and resources given him to grow his investment. Likewise, we are often deprived of our divine inheritance because we've "sized it up" and determined it is not worth our time or attention. Those with ten and five bags of money were assigned leadership positions. The man with one bag of money ended up with less than what he had at the start.

Up To the Minute

There are several practical steps that you can implement into your life and work to ensure that you honor the time God has allotted you. Among the most important are punctuality, schedule consideration, and flexibility maintenance.

Punctuality:

Punctuality is a vital consideration for communication that one should practice as much as possible. At the end of any meeting you are conducting, when you announce the next meeting, ensure that everyone clearly understands the next meeting's date and time. Then, remember to respect everyone else's time by showing up promptly yourself – preferably earlier, considering the time you need for set up.

Schedule Consideration:

Consider the schedules of others when setting dates and times for meetings. Of course, it's a given that all participants may not be able to accommodate every proposed meeting time. Still, considering the lives and demands of your teammates demonstrates your willingness to work with your group. Such considerations should, in turn, increase their desire to work with you as well.

Maintain Flexibility:

While structure is crucial, it is equally essential to fortify that structure with the balance of flexibility. For example, the newer high-rises built in Los Angeles are very structurally sound, but the architects designed them to bend and flex during earthquakes. This flexibility causes them to withstand the effects of earthquakes better.[153] Rigid, inflexible schedules do not result in cooperation. As we see in Ecclesiastes, times change, and we also must be willing to change with the times. Always remember the scripture that says, "Blessed are the flexible, for they shall not break." (2 Sharon 3:29, Revised Williams Version).

Stick To the Program

One key ingredient for maximizing your time during meetings is to create a well-planned agenda. An agenda provides a visible platform for the structure of your session. The most effective meetings in the corporate world typically adhere to the guidelines of an agenda. Agendas help us focus on tasks at hand while streamlining the meeting process to adhere to meeting timeframes. When formulating an agenda, keep in mind that you should follow the agenda's flow as much as possible unless the Holy Spirit leads you to go in another direction.

What do you do if you've completed all the items on the agenda early? In the spirit of involving God in everything, remember you have allotted this time to His service, so use it to serve Him. In a church setting, consider using any spare time for prayer, Bible study, or sharing testimonials of what God is doing in the lives of meeting participants.

Many people prefer rushing ahead to tend to other personal duties even though they've set that time aside for kingdom work. As leaders that God has chosen, wouldn't it be nice to condition your team to dedicate the entire time of this meeting to the service of God? Wouldn't it be refreshing to devote the remaining time to address spiritual fulfillment?

If you are in a corporate setting, consider releasing the group early to provide them with extra time to complete assigned tasks. During that time, you can steal away to seek God for more spirit-led direction.

Alternatively, what if the meeting is running longer than anticipated? Again, we must remember to consider the schedules of others. In today's society, many people have full plates with or without your meeting. In the spirit of cooperation, consider adjourning and discuss setting another date to continue discussions unless everyone agrees to stay longer. Suppose the meeting topic is rated high on God's list of priorities. In that case, you may be pleasantly surprised that the group would often rather sacrifice other obligations to tend to God's business right then and there.

While God wonderfully created times and seasons, *we* determine whether *The Calendar Principle* will work for or against us. For those of us who struggle in these areas – myself included – let us learn to discipline ourselves so that we can ensure that time is on our side.

Key Takeaways:

→ God often redeems missed opportunities, but not always. Therefore, it is critical to take advantage of time and opportunities based on the Holy Spirit's leading.

→ God doesn't need time, but we do. God has given us time to reconnect with Him through salvation, to fulfill purpose, and to seize on opportunities.

→ As leaders, we must strive to improve time management through punctuality, maintaining flexibility, and considering the schedules of others.

Reflections:

→ How would you describe your previous time management skills?

→ How can those skills be improved?

→ How well do you stick to agendas that you have created?

Prayer:

Heavenly Father, I thank You for the time You've given me to fulfill Your purpose on this earth. Please forgive me for squandered or mishandled time, and grant me the wisdom to redeem time lost. Please teach me how to implement practical time-management tools so that I can maximize the time You've allotted for me to fulfill Your will. This I ask in Jesus' Name, as I praise you. AMEN!

Chapter 12

THE KNOWLEDGE PRINCIPLE

Who Is That Masked Man?

How much better is it to get wisdom than gold! and to get understanding rather to be chosen than silver!
(Proverbs 16:16)

Then Eliashib the high priest rose up with his brethren the priests, and they builded the sheep gate; they sanctified it, and set up the doors of it; even unto the tower of Meah they sanctified it, unto the tower of Hananel.
(Nehemiah 3:1)

A s stated in *The Foundation Principle*, Nehemiah chapter three reflects how well Nehemiah knew his team. His knowledge of his worker's capabilities equipped him to build successfully. He tapped into *The Knowledge Principle*: Knowledge is Power, and the lack of knowledge can lead to ruin. Hence, Proverbs 4:7 tells us:

> **Wisdom is the principal thing, therefore get wisdom, and with all thy getting, get understanding.**

Hosea shows us the consequences of not harnessing the power that knowledge wields by prophesying:

> **My people are destroyed for lack of knowledge: because thou hast rejected knowledge, I will also reject thee, that thou shalt be no priest to me: seeing thou hast forgotten the law of thy God, I will also forget thy children.**
>
> **(Hosea 4:6)**

Know Them

Understanding the importance of *The Knowledge Principle*, Paul had this to say to the church of Thessalonica:

> **Now also we beseech you, brethren, get to know those who labor among you [recognize them for what they are, acknowledge and appreciate and respect them all] ...**
>
> **(1 Thessalonians 5:12a, AMP)**

How well did Nehemiah know those who labored with him? Let's take King Artaxerxes, for example. Nehemiah had been planning for months before the king inquired of his countenance. Had Nehemiah not known the king or his culture, he might not have waited for the king to ask him why he was sad to broach the subject. Nehemiah knew the potential danger of not waiting for the king to open the door for negotiations. Conversely, suppose Nehemiah didn't have a close relationship with the king. In that case, he might not have been bold enough to ask the king for traveling papers, let alone the materials he would need to begin rebuilding.

Most importantly, Nehemiah knew his God. He knew whom to seek first. On the other hand, the king may not have known Nehemiah's God, but he *did* know Nehemiah. Not only had his reputation preceded him, but he had developed a relationship of trust with the king also. Had the king not known Nehemiah, he may well have refused his request, thereby thwarting his mission.

Additionally, working closely with people of other nationalities creates an atmosphere whereby one can study the cultures of others. The more we learn about the cultures of our colleagues, the better we understand their mindsets, belief systems, and social cues.

Finally, the people we know best are most often immediate family members. I'm sure that Nehemiah knew his brother Hanani better than anyone else. Hanani arrived in Jerusalem before Nehemiah. He was the one who alerted Nehemiah of the condition there. Nehemiah knew Hanani's values, discipline, and love of country. He also knew that Hanani was "more faithful and God-fearing above many."[154] Therefore, when they finished building the wall, Nehemiah assigned Hanani to one of the two lieutenant governor positions.

Today, many people would cry foul and accuse Nehemiah of nepotism. However, scholars believe that Nehemiah hired Hanani in preparation for his return to his post in the Persian Court.[155] Nehemiah still worked for King Artaxerxes, and he didn't ask for a permanent relocation. Thus, he needed to ensure that someone he trusted would continue the job he began.

The Cultural Connection

Before entering full-time ministry, I was a training manager at a major Japanese-owned telecommunications company that sold high-end telecommunications solutions. I've seen sales ranging anywhere from $30,000 to more than $2 million.

During one of the sales classes I facilitated, our guest speaker – responsible for foreign relations – shared some sales "no-no's" when dealing with Japanese clients. She related that when a Japanese businessman receives a business card, he studies it. He reads the entire front and then checks the back to see if it contains any written messages. When he gives his business card out, he often writes a unique thought on the back. He then observes the recipient as he reads the card. Not taking the time to study his business card is often viewed as a capital offense to the Japanese businessman. The offended party will never disclose the violation. He will simply take his business elsewhere. Many account executives have lost potential customers and revenue without knowing the cause.

Culture plays an integral role in learning about your colleagues. Few people realize that culture extends far beyond ethnic backgrounds. In the United States, some people assume that race is the only aspect of culture. Yet, there are a wide variety of subcultures within and between races. For example, the deaf community comprises all races but has a culture of its own. Geographically, we have various subcultures. Due to the media's heavy influence on society, western culture often transcends race, but not necessarily location. Once you leave the west, you depart from the culture of the west.

Even though images portraying various cultures in the USA directly influence many South African people, I had to adapt to their culture. While our culture influences them, they haven't adopted many of our traditions into their lives. They don't understand many of our traditions.

Case in point: During my first winter in South Africa, I was astounded by how everyone wore winter coats inside their homes. I would watch in amazement as women cooked over gas stoves while their coat sleeves danced around the fire. I didn't realize that most people in South Africa don't have the luxury of central heating, so indoor coats are their norm. On the other hand, wearing a coat inside is a form of bondage to me, so I continued my practice of removing my coat and snuggling up under a blanket.

When I explained this to my good friend, Mbulelo, his eyes bulged as a lightbulb went off in his head. He said, "Wow! Whenever I watched people remove their coats while indoors on American TV shows, I would think that those guys were mad! Why in the world would they take their coats off in such cold weather? Don't they realize they can catch the flu?" Indoor coats are a thing there. Stripping out of coats indoors is a thing here.

Within the body of Christ are a host of cultures also. Denominations are often segregated by culture. Within denominations, subcultures exist between various local and area assemblies and ministries. Within local congregations, you often find clicks that morph into more subcultures as well.

While we were all created in God's image and likeness, I believe He created us all to be different to reflect the multiple facets of His glory. Therefore, it is essential to learn about, respect, and appreciate other cultures. I'm sure if you study long enough, you'll find at least one aspect of God's glory revealed that you've never noticed before in every culture you explore. I am not implying that one must embrace cultural beliefs that contradict the word of God. But one mustn't judge and condemn others for their cultural beliefs, especially if you don't know the context or origin. Gaining an understanding of why those beliefs exist may be the very tool God uses to bring those souls to Christ through you.

Who's Who

It is also essential to recognize **who** it is that labors among us. When we say "get to know the people you work with," one may assume that this rule is limited to peers only. Yet, in 1 Thessalonians 5:12, Paul identifies superiors when he says:

> **And we beseech you, brethren, to know them which labour among you, and are over you in the Lord, and admonish you (emphasis added).**

Superiors and subordinates are also co-laborers, as they are involved in business, ministry, or project success. Remember that Nehemiah and King Artaxerxes were not only acquainted; they knew each other well. The better you get to know others, the easier it is to fulfill 1 Thessalonians 5:13, which says:

> **And to esteem them very highly in love for their work's sake. And be at peace among yourselves.**

As you learn your co-laborers' personality, culture, and spirit, it becomes easier to honor them for their labors. It will also be easier to keep the peace because you can more readily prepare to identify how to handle conflicts that may arise through discernment.

Discernment peels back the mask of surface connection and communication. By peeling back the mask, you reveal the essence of the person. It is ingrained in us as humans to always "put our best foot forward," especially in public. But anyone who lives with others will tell you that the person they live with wears a mask to hide facets of their true selves when they leave the door of their home.

We find a great example of this in kids. When I was a teenager, no one in my house knew that I smoked marijuana and cigarettes. I cursed like a sailor. But *never* at home. I was in my 40s when I finally told one of my sisters about getting high. My family knew I was moody, but none of them had a clue that I spent most of my teen years depressed and even suicidal in my early teens. Knowing nothing about how to tap into the spirit of discernment, not only did they not know me, they had no idea that they didn't know me.

Solomon's prayer in 1 Kings provides insight into another way that the spirit-filled believer can stir up the gift of discernment. While he was praying, God asked him what he desired. God did not place any stipulations upon His request.

Solomon's experience reminds me of the old genie in a bottle tale which only gives three wishes. When the genie granted those wishes, the master had to live with those wishes and their consequences. In this story, however, there is no make-believe genie. The Lord God Jehovah himself was ready to grant any request Solomon could think of, consequence-free. Many people would target temporary fulfillment such as lovely homes or cars, debt cancellation, love, romance, and other things that endure but for a moment. While there is nothing wrong with those things, Solomon's request surpassed his selfish desires.

> **Give therefore thy servant an *understanding heart* to judge thy people, that I may *discern between good and bad*: for who is able to judge this thy so great a people?**
>
> **(1 Kings 3:9, emphasis added)**

What a simple request! Solomon only wanted wisdom from God to discern good from evil, which is how discernment differs from perception. Tapping into God's wisdom and hearing His voice empowers us to discern. Through our desire to get wisdom, all else will follow. Thus, Solomon's instruction to us:

> **Wisdom [is] the principal thing; [therefore] get wisdom: and with all thy getting get understanding.**
>
> **(Proverbs 4:7)**

The Spirit of A Man

Have you ever met a lovely couple who fits this description? Married for more than 30 years, they can often complete each other's sentences. They seem to know each other's thoughts. They are the epitome of one flesh. They seem to flow in a rhythm. They've learned each other's spirit through years of intimacy. They've obviously spent a lot of quality time together. You don't have to be married for 30 years to "know them that labor among you," but you do have to spend quality time with them to learn their spirits.

Unfortunately, in most cases, this is the exception, not the rule. Have you ever heard people declare that they know you after being in your presence for a short period of time? Meanwhile, you found yourself wondering if the person even knows you from Adam? I've been in situations where I spent long periods with people who declared that they knew me very well, but from their actions, I knew that they had no clue who I really was.

Let's ponder a couple of other true-to-life scenarios. Consider the man who finds himself in shock after many years of marriage because his wife files for divorce. He feels like he has been kicked in the gut because he never saw it coming. Meanwhile, the wife believes that had he taken the time to listen to her to really know her, he would have realized how unhappy she was.

Or, consider the ministry that dissolved because the partners thought they knew each other well, only to find out that they did not know each other at all. This lack of knowledge is often the context for which many churches and other ministries have split.

We become victims to such scenarios because we assume that we know people based on our early perceptions of personality traits, mannerisms, and behavioral patterns. Yet, to effectively lead, it is crucial to learn not just personalities and behaviors but also the spirit of those with whom we labor.

Quickly ascertaining if someone is generous, sociable, or quick-tempered is usually an effortless task. But at this level, we've only scratched the surface by learning that person's personality. A surface level of knowledge can give us a false sense of in-depth understanding of the person we are "getting to know."

It is more important and often more challenging to ascertain what is operating beyond the person's psyche. What triggers behavior? What is behind personality traits? We must push past the soul (i.e., mind, will, and emotions) and become sensitive to our co-laborers' spirits. To do this, we must learn to peel back the surface layer of their physical flesh and the psychological inner workings of their mind to expose the meat of their spirit.

Nehemiah took this principle further by discerning his enemies' spirit after the enemy was planted directly inside the camp. Shemaiah was the son of a priest, and apparently, a self-proclaimed prophet. Nehemiah went to visit him because he had placed himself in home confinement. Shemaiah suggested that Nehemiah accompany him by shutting himself into the temple to protect him from the "enemy." Then, to instill a spirit of fear, Shemaiah claimed that the enemy "will come and slay thee." But the "enemy" was within. Nehemiah perceived that Sanballat and Tobiah hired Shemaiah and others as a lure to distract from completing the wall and rejected his advice.[156] Had Nehemiah not discerned Shemaiah's spirit, project delays or abandonment would have resulted.

Knowing that the Jews sought to kill him for claiming to be equal with God, Jesus made a fascinating statement:

> *You study the Scriptures, because you think that in them you will find eternal life. And these very Scriptures speak about me! Yet you are not willing to come to me in order to have life.*
>
> **(John 5:39-40, GNB, emphasis added)**

In so many words, Jesus told them the same thing he told Phillip in John 14:9 when Phillip asked Him to show him the Father. He said,

> *"Have I been with you so long, and you still do not know me, Philip? Whoever has seen me has seen the Father. How can you say, 'Show us the Father'?"*
>
> **(John 14:9, ESV)**

Phillip was one of the original 12 disciples. He spent three years "getting to know" Jesus during His ministry. Yet, he still did not realize that to know Jesus *was* to know the Father. Likewise, the Jews who spent their lives studying the scriptures hoping to gain eternal life wanted to kill the eternal Life-Giver. Why? Because they never got the chance to know His Spirit.

During the three years that Phillip followed Jesus, he witnessed the miracles. He observed Jesus' prayer life. He heard the sermons. He knew about Jesus' encounter with the Samaritan woman at the well who asked Him for the living waters that would eternally quench her thirst. [157] Yet, Jesus easily perceived that in all that time, Phillip hadn't gotten to know His Spirit.

How much we trust God is a direct reflection of how well we think we know Him. Conversely, how much we trust people is based on how much we think we know them. If you do not know those you are working with, how do you know you can trust them? How do you know that if you give them an assignment, they will carry it through? How will you know when it's time for the professional aspect of the relationship to end? How do you know that they won't turn around and stab you in the back?

We don't know everything, and we won't see everything coming, but warning precedes destruction when we tune our ears into God's frequency.[158] Therefore, we must spend time sharpening our spirit of discernment to learn the spirits of those with whom we are co-laboring.

We must keep the gift of discernment stirred up to accurately discern the spirits that influence and motivate our co-laborers. This discernment, in turn, will give us the ability to make wise decisions and respond appropriately to the actions of others.

How do we tap into the spirit of Discernment? The answer to this question requires a bit of examination. Thus, we will dive into the spirit of discernment next.

Meanwhile, let's not forget that God's wisdom transcends culture, behavior, belief systems, and spirits. Therefore, let us remember to seek the wisdom of God to discern so that we can uncover that masked man.

Key Takeaways:

→ The lack of knowledge can lead to ruin. Therefore, seeking wisdom in every aspect of one's endeavor is a must.

→ Great leaders take the time to know their colleagues on a social, cultural, and spiritual level regardless of role or position.

→ The most intimate knowledge one can learn of another is their spirit through discernment.

Reflections:

→ Consider how well you know your current colleagues. Then, on a colleague-by-colleague basis, consider what steps you can take to get to know them better?

→ Reflect on times when you experienced cultural barriers that resulted in conflict. How did you resolve the dispute?

→ Can you name anyone outside of your immediate family whose spirit you've successfully discerned? If so, how did you cultivate your discernment skills in that instance?

Prayer:

Beloved King of Kings, thank You for knowing me for who I am. Thank You for creating me in Your image and likeness. Just as You know my spirit, show me both Your Spirit and my co-laborers' spirits. Teach me to learn them so that I may work in harmony with them and be an example that illustrates Your love, mercy, and grace. Where I lack understanding of cultural differences, grant me the favor to learn those differences and grow so that I can be a beacon of life and hope to others regardless of ethnic differences. This I ask and trust You to answer, in Jesus' name. AMEN!

Chapter 13

TO DISCERN OR NOT TO DISCERN

THAT IS THE QUESTION

---

*For the word of God is quick, and powerful, and sharper than
any twoedged sword, piercing even to the dividing asunder
of soul and spirit, and of the joints and marrow, and is a
discerner of the thoughts and intents of the heart.*
(Hebrews 4:12)

*And I discerned, and, lo, God had not sent him; for he pronounced this
prophecy against me, whereas Tobiah and Sanballat had hired him.
(Nehemiah 6:12, Jewish Publication Society Old Testament)*

B y now, you've learned several principles you can use to develop your leadership skills through discipline, focus, determination, self-introspection, and wisdom from God. Applying discernment to every principle presented throughout this book will exponentially strengthen your leadership capabilities. To that end, let's explore how to sharpen your sense of discernment by intensifying your mastery of these principles through *stirring the flame*.

The World's Greatest Flame Thrower

My first vacation to Jamaica in 1993 provided me with a few exciting firsts in my life. This trip was my first exposure to cultures not easily accessible in the US. I also enjoyed my first snorkeling experience, which opened the door to several delightful years of scuba diving and my first invitation to the United Kingdom. A friend and I gladly accepted the invitation to celebrate our college graduations. Furthermore, my first all-inclusive hotel stay opened the door for me to enjoy some spectacular shows.

One show, in particular, showcased a fantastic flame thrower. This man performed all types of stunts and dances -- including the Limbo – while tossing flames here and there. As dangerous as fire can be in and of itself, there appeared to be not one strand of hair, article of clothing, prop, or flesh damaged during the show. His ability to ignite and then control flames was fascinating, to say the least.

Now, let's time travel back to the day of Pentecost, shortly after Jesus' ascension.[159] When the Holy Spirit descended, tongue-shaped flames appeared and rested on the Disciples. They instantly began speaking in tongues as the Holy Spirit filled their very spirits.[160] Likewise, when God's spirit enters our being, His Spirit's flame ignites ours by re-linking our spirits with God's. When this happens, the Holy Spirit grants us direct access to the throne room of God through our ever-eternal High Priest, Jesus Christ.[161]

Prior to the day of Pentecost, only the fallible high priest had access to the Holy of Holies, or God's throne room, once per year.[162] Since then, the Holy Spirit has given us our prayer language (tongues) that we can use to petition God directly in His "courtroom" anytime day or night. In 1 Corinthians 14:2, Paul teaches us that even though our minds cannot comprehend what we are saying, our spirits speak mysteries when we speak in tongues. When we no longer know how to pray in our native language, we release the Holy Spirit to intercede for us through our prayer language. Paul explains it in his letter to the church in Rome like this:

> **So too the [Holy] Spirit comes to our aid and bears us up in our weakness; for we do not know what prayer to offer nor how to offer it worthily as we ought, but the Spirit Himself goes to meet our supplication and pleads in our behalf with unspeakable yearnings and groanings too deep for utterance.**
>
> **(Romans 8:26, AMP)**

Praying in tongues charges the battery of our spirit, as His flame energizes our spiritual senses.[163] When I commune with God in tongues, I've noticed that my spiritual ears become tuned into God's heart. At these times, I begin to hear Him provide me with direction, correction, and encouragement. When I don't know how to pray for a person or situation, I pray in tongues. Typically, I will hear a word, feel an impression, or see a vision of the problem during this time, which drives how I pray in English. I will often receive prophetic words to speak over the lives of others through intercession. At other times,

God will give me a prophetic word to speak directly to people. Praying in tongues is the only time I don't have to think before I speak.

The World's Greatest Flame Grower

Once we receive our prayer language, we can use it to activate the nine spiritual gifts addressed in 1 Corinthians chapter 12. Paul said this gift package "is given to each one for the common good."[164] Included is the gift of discernment.

Of all the incidents I experienced in which discernment led to a breakthrough, one stands out the most. It happened at a restaurant during lunch with someone with whom I had devoted much of my time. Callie and I were colleagues who had known each other for decades. While we were silently eating, the Lord allowed me to listen in on a conversation He started with Callie. He asked her about elevating me to a specific leadership position. She physically grunted, "hmmm!" as she began complaining about me to the Lord in her spirit. After hearing Callie's spirit respond to the Lord replete with an audible grunt, I asked, "what was that "hmmm" for?"

"Oh, nothing," she replied.

"No! Tell me! What was that "hmmm" for?"

"I just had a crazy thought," she said, having no idea I heard the entire conversation.

She had no clue that God was moving me in a different direction. As a matter of fact, until that moment, I didn't realize it either. While God had been gently hinting to me that He had other things in mind for me, I was a bit slow to get the hint. My devotion up to that point was greater for Callie than for God, but I hadn't realized it. You can bet your bottom dollar I got the hint that day! Little did I know that Callie wasn't satisfied with me because God had His own plans for me.

Several months later, God, who is faithful to confirm His word, did just that. One day, Callie mentioned that she had entertained the thought of placing me in a key position. By then, it was too late. I had moved on. That incident was pivotal in my transition to relocate to South Africa. God stirred up the gift of discernment in me as a part of my "missionary training" through my intimacy with Him.

Convinced that Timothy had the gift of faith, Apostle Paul admonished him to stir up the spiritual gift residing in him.[165] The phrase "stir up" is derived from the Greek word, "anazōpureō," which literally means "to kindle up a dormant fire."[166] But there is no way to rekindle a flame that has never existed. (If you have not received your flame yet, don't fret. I'll discuss how to spark that flame later.)

Paul encouraged Timothy to fan the flame of the Holy Spirit, which like embers, needs an accelerant to grow and produce new flames. Tongues are a spiritual accelerant. When you worship in your prayer language, you are pouring your accelerant into the fire, which is the Holy Spirit. Likewise, you are activating and developing the "spiritual gift package" residing in your spirit, thus "growing your flame." Growing your flame gives you access to the nine gifts of the spirit listed in 1 Corinthians chapter 12.

While sharpened spiritual senses seem to come easy to some, others have difficulty tapping into the gifts. The key to stirring up those gifts is intimacy with Jesus. There are 1,440 minutes in a 24-hour period. Ask yourself: "How much time do I spend on personal devotions, study, or prayer? If your answer is 3-5 minutes a day, then there's a chance you'll struggle to tap into or develop your spiritual gifts.

Most married people will agree that constant, consistent communication is the key to a successful marriage. As I pointed out in *The Knowledge Principle*, the more time you spend with your spouse, the better you'll get to know that person. I once heard a beloved sister say, "If you devote only one hour to Him, He will take care of the other 23."

Before the advent of electronic Bibles and smartphones, I recall someone else asking the question, "Do you want to hear God's voice?" She then picked up a bible with both hands, held it sideways, and repeatedly opened and closed it, saying, "Then you have to open up His mouth."

We often forget that the Bible *is* the Word of God. By studying it, we learn the mind of Christ. Spending intimate time in personal Bible study teaches us how to pray His will and train our ears to hear His voice. By adding prayer – in your prayer language and your native tongue – and Bible study, you ignite the intimacy which stirs up the gift of God in you. Here is a great equation to apply to your daily life:

$$
\begin{aligned}
&\text{Worship} \\
+\ &\text{Word} \\
+\ &\text{Prayer} \\
\hline
=\ &\textit{Intimacy}
\end{aligned}
$$

$$\textit{Intimacy} = \textit{Spiritual Gift Activation}$$

Don't despair if you do not feel you've experienced discernment or the wonderful world of Holy Spirit infilling. The next chapter is devoted to providing you with all you need to enjoy this gift package created especially for you.

Key Takeaways:

→ The Holy Spirit is a flame that God deposits into the spirits of those who grant Him entrance. Thus, stirring up the gift of God means to fan the embers of the dormant fire of the Holy Spirit, which activates spiritual gifts.

→ When we speak in tongues, Jesus intercedes on our behalf.

→ Intimacy is a requirement for flowing in the gifts of the Spirit, including discernment.

Reflections:

→ Have you ever fanned the flames of the Holy Spirit? If so, how did (or do) you stir up your gifts of the Spirit?

→ Reflect on experiences in which you wish you had discerned others' spirits. How do you think the course of events could have changed had you tapped into that gift?

→ If you have discerned spirits in the past, think back to determine the correlation between your intimacy in devotion and the intensity of discernment you experienced. If you haven't re-ignited those flames recently, take some time to do so now.

Prayer:

Precious Lord, I thank You for the gifts You have all wrapped up and ready to deliver to Your children. Unlike Santa Claus, I thank You that You are authentic and Your gifts are eternal. Please grace me with my prayer language and stir it up in me so that I can stay energized with Power from on High. Develop the spirit of discernment in me so that I can be used for Your glory to be a blessing to others, in Jesus' name, AMEN!

Chapter 14

BE KIND, REWIND

For through him we both have access by one Spirit unto the Father. Now therefore ye are no more strangers and foreigners, but fellowcitizens with the saints, and of the household of God; And are built upon the foundation of the apostles and prophets, Jesus Christ himself being the chief corner stone; In whom all the building fitly framed together groweth unto an holy temple in the Lord: In whom ye also are builded together for an habitation of God through the Spirit.
(Ephesians 2:18-22)

... For all the people wept, when they heard the words of the law.
(Nehemiah 8:9b)

Those of us who lived through the VHS years had the privilege of renting movies from video rental shops. Unlike DVD technology, VHS tapes required what sometimes felt like a lengthy rewinding process. Many people would agree that the last thing one desired to do was impatiently wait while a newly rented video rewound from the end to the beginning of the tape. Hence, many video rental shops began posting signs that read, "BE KIND, REWIND," and this is what we will do right now.

Thus far, we have explored ten principles used to develop Godly, effective leaders. Moreover, we provided the key to unlocking the power to maximize the use of those principles. There is one final key left to collect, however. Accessing this key will equip you to harness enough spiritual power to implement the principles to their fullest capacity. To gain access to this key, I must begin with issues concerning study.

Study Hiccups

I've always been told that the Bible never contradicts itself. I have concluded from my personal studies that this is indeed the case. While several variables exist that causes Biblical contradictions, the three greatest culprits that I've observed are:

1. Varied interpretations based on flawed study methods.
2. Inappropriate approaches for proving hypotheses.
3. Revelation rejection.

Flawed Study Methods:

During *The Knowledge Principle* discussion, I quoted John 5:39, where Jesus told the Jews to search the scriptures. The Jews didn't recognize

Jesus as their Messiah because they studied scripture erroneously. Their eyes were blinded because Jesus didn't match their ill-conceived notions of the Messiah even though He met the description to a "T."

It is often easy to study without employing proper study tools, which creates challenges when reconciling perceived scripture inconsistencies. Language, context, customs, contrasts, and comparisons are snippets of the varied approaches to in-depth Bible study. Sometimes, we can become so focused on answers that we inadvertently skip crucial pieces of the study puzzle. Yet, upon further examination, we find that the conclusions we've drawn seem to cause scriptural clashes.

For example, I often heard the doctrine that there are no dogs in heaven during my time abroad. I then began to observe how people would mistreat dogs. Many dogs didn't usually receive much attention or compassion from their owners. As an animal lover, the mistreatment would grieve me.

The only scripture I found that they could base this teaching on is Revelation 22:16, which lists those who forfeit the right to enter heaven. Dogs are at the top of the list, followed by sorcerers, the sexually immoral, murderers, idolaters, and liars. Except for dogs, the common thread is that all the others that are listed are humans.

I struggled with this doctrine because it singles out dogs. I have never heard anyone speak this way about snakes, or scorpions, or any other animal for that matter, having souls or residing in heaven. I also struggled to reconcile that view with Isaiah 65:17-25, where God describes the new heavens and earth. Note how the prophecy ends:

> **The wolf and the lamb shall feed together, and the lion shall eat straw like the bullock: and dust *shall be* the serpent's meat. They shall not hurt nor destroy in all my holy mountain, saith the LORD.**
>
> **(Isaiah 65:25)**

The potential for confusion stemming from the word "dogs" prompted me to investigate further. I knew that throughout scripture, some people were called dogs. Mephibosheth referred to himself as a dead dog. Hazael called himself a dog. Abishai called Shimei a dog. Jesus all but outright called a Syrophoenician woman a dog, and Paul warned the Philippians to beware of dogs.[167]

In fact, out of the 41 times scripture cites the word "dog," 27 instances were figurative or in comparison to dogs. The literal references are of dogs eating or human interaction with canines. Further research revealed that people in the Jewish culture referred to gentiles or miscreants as dogs during those times.[168] It took in-depth word and cultural background studies to expose the error in that doctrine.

Inappropriate Approach Used To Prove Hypotheses:

My doctor recommended that I consider changing my dietary habits to a low-carb or Ketogenic lifestyle to combat a very little-known diagnosis. When I shared that I was considering switching to Keto, someone cautioned me because she assumed that low-carb eating adversely affected her kidneys. Soon after, I began hearing people warn about how Keto is unhealthy for your cholesterol. Thus, I started my research as I shifted my eating habits.

As I was growing up, doctors universally taught that saturated fat increases instances of heart disease by raising the amount of "bad" cholesterol in the blood. The American Heart Association warned through TV ads to avoid foods like eggs, red meat, and butter. In time, the low-fat diet became the focus. Unknowingly, our society embraced the guidance and began swapping out fats for carbs and seed oils. Since then, rates of chronic illness and obesity have skyrocketed.

In 2015, the Dietary Guidelines Advisory Committee concluded that dietary cholesterol such as saturated fat ***does not*** affect blood cholesterol. The methods used in the 1950s studies were flawed, and people worldwide have paid a hefty price.[169]

One trap that is easy to fall into is attempting to compel scripture to align with your hypothesis. One should ***never*** single out scripture to force it to conform to a theory. A hypothesis is just that – a theory, but the Bible is truth. Thus, one must always test hypotheses ***against*** the Bible. Never attempt to make the Bible measure up to theory. Instead, test all theories to determine whether they measure up to Bible truths. If they do not, then discard the theory as false.

I've often heard people partially quote Psalms 37:4 as if God granting our desires is an unconditional promise. They would stand on that promise as if their lives depended on it without bothering to consider their lifestyles. The verse begins with, "Delight yourself in the Lord." The promise is conditional. If God were to give anyone who knows this scripture their heart's desires without condition, all dogs – pun intended – ***will*** go to heaven. By ignoring the condition, many people erroneously use the Bible to justify their theories.

Revelation Rejection:

The Apostle Paul said that we only know "in part." He describes our understanding as looking through a dark glass. [170] We only understand the part of scripture that we know through revelation. The trap of believing we have mastered scriptural knowledge leads to stunted growth.

Earlier, I cited that one of the issues in understanding scripture was flawed study methods, whereby critical information is omitted when forming a deduction. However, this is an intellectual approach to study. While it is essential to factor in every aspect of the study, one must be careful not to elevate detailed findings above revelation.

When God breathes illumination upon scripture, the recipients of the revelation often experience rejection and sometimes even abuse because their audiences' natural minds cannot comprehend the revelation. People who do not understand revelation tend to kill the revelator. The Jews killed Jesus because they *thought* they knew the scripture. These were highly intellectual men who studied scripture from cover to cover as their occupations. They were waiting for the eternal life-giver to come. Yet, they failed to recognize Him when He arrived. Thus, they killed the eternal-life giver that they were anxiously awaiting.

Martin Luther's doctrine of salvation through faith by grace resulted in his excommunication from the Catholic church.[171] They couldn't support his doctrine because God didn't reveal it to them. As of today, the Catholic doctrine of salvation remains works-based.[172]

What's That You Say?

There is much debate within the Christian community surrounding the subject of speaking in tongues. Some people believe that the events in the book of Acts do not apply to people today. Others believe that the Holy Spirit is a gift available to those who want Him, albeit unnecessary. There's also the doctrine that tongues are not proof of being filled with the Holy Spirit. Instead, this doctrine suggests that we are Spirit-filled through repentance (or "the Sinner's Prayer"). Still, others teach that it is a necessity, part of the "new birth" process.

Fortunately, I didn't know any of these schools of thought when I experienced the infilling of the Holy Spirit. Therefore, I couldn't be swayed by any specific doctrine. My personal experience taught me that hunger for a relationship with God and willingness to devote one's life to the Lord entirely creates the perfect atmosphere for Holy Spirit infilling.

After praying the prayer of repentance, I felt the urge to thank the Lord continuously. I kept repeating, "Thank You, Jesus," because that was all I knew to say. My heart became hungry, and my mind became focused on worshiping Him. Literally within moments, I enjoyed the same experience that the disciples enjoyed on the day of Pentecost in Acts chapter 2 simply by vocally praising Him with my whole heart. I did not just appreciate Him with my lips. I longed for Him with my very being, and suddenly it happened! I literally felt what seemed like a warm yet strong breath enter my body through my mouth to my core as my words transformed from English to a language I did not know. In that split second, it was as if there was a fire placed inside me, driving me to serve God with unspeakable joy and hunger to know Him more intimately.[173]

After my Holy Ghost experience, I became exposed to the various schools of thought concerning the new birth process. Therefore, I began to study for myself. I had no intention to prove or disprove any one particular doctrine. My chief goal was to uncover the truth that I could scripturally confirm without contradictions. Low and behold, my conclusion appeared to meet that criterion.

The following is a condensed version of the conclusion of my study.

In John chapter 3, a Jewish ruler named Nicodemus approached Jesus, acknowledging that He was a teacher that God sent. Jesus's reply seemed odd. He said:

Truly, truly, I say to you, unless one is born again, he cannot see the Kingdom of God.

(John 3:3, ESV, emphasis added)

Here He acknowledged that we must be born again. Note, however, that He only gave the prescription for *seeing* the Kingdom of God.

I'm sure that Nicodemus was perplexed by such a paradoxical statement coming from Jesus. So he asked how such a thing could happen. "Can he squeeze his supersized self back into his mother's womb then pop back out a second time?" (Sharon's Revised Version, of course).

I've heard many people teach that repentance is the act of being born again. Yet, this is only the first portion of the equation. Jesus' reply holds the key to unlocking what I call "the Birthing Equation":

Truly, truly, I say to you, unless one is born of water and the Spirit, he cannot enter the Kingdom of God.

(John 3:5, ESV, emphasis added)

Thus, Jesus provided Nicodemus (and us) with the formula:

Born Again

\+ Born of Water

\+ Born Of Spirit

———————————

= **New Birth**

We now face the challenge that Jesus only provided us with a formula that some may view as cryptic. He didn't spell out what Born Again, Born of Water, or Born of Spirit means. Jesus then continues by distinguishing between being born again and, well … being born again by describing the make-up of our natural and spiritual births.

> **That which is born of the flesh is flesh, and that which is born of the Spirit is spirit.**
>
> **(John 3:6, ESV)**

Next, He emphasizes its importance for the third time.

> **Do not marvel that I said to you, 'You must be born again.'**
>
> **(John 3:7, ESV)**

Finally, He provides an analogy to describe what it is like to be born of the Spirit, or Spirit-filled.

> **The wind blows where it wishes, and you hear its sound, but you do not know where it comes from or where it goes. So it is with everyone who is born of the Spirit."**
>
> **(John 3:8, ESV)**

Shortly before His crucifixion, Jesus told His disciples that He would leave them but would eventually return. But in the interim, He promised to pray that the Father would send them (and us) another Comforter which He referred to as the "Spirit of Truth," if we obey His commandments.[174] What did Jesus command His disciples? He commanded that they be born again, of water and the Spirit according to John 3:3-8.

Have you ever been in a class where the lecture was so confusing that you didn't even know what question to ask because you were so lost? I bet that's how Nicodemus and Jesus' disciples must have felt after hearing Jesus' words. I can picture the disciples scratching their heads thinking: *First, He said we must be born again, whatever that means, but He doesn't tell us how to do this born-again thingy. Now, He's promising to pray for God to send some other guy that will not only live with us but would live in us also. Huh?*

Still, Jesus just wouldn't quit piling on the "riddles." Later, in John 14:18-20, He told His disciples that when the Comforter comes, they would know that Jesus is "in the Father, and ye in me, and I in you." *How on God's green earth could this be possible?* Ok, any more head-scratching, and I'd question if the disciples needed an anti-dandruff shampoo.

Jesus then made another promise when He appeared to the disciples after His resurrection that, "ye shall receive power, after that the Holy Ghost is come upon you."[175] Then, in Acts, chapter 2, Jesus kept His promises which turned out to be one and the same. That's when the disciples finally understood the answer to all His cryptic explanations.

While they were praising God together, "They saw what seemed to be tongues of fire that separated and came to rest on each of them."[176] Then they were all instantly "filled with the Holy Spirit, and they began to speak different languages. Throughout the book of Acts, the Holy Spirit filled the spiritually hungry with Himself and all the power that He harnesses.[177]

The evidence of God filling them with the power of the Holy Ghost was speaking foreign languages they did not know. People from 15 different countries heard them speaking in their respective languages. Instead of wondering how these Jews could suddenly praise God in their languages, they assumed that the disciples were either crazy or drunk. To set them straight, Peter preached his first sermon ever without one ounce of preparation – yet another promise Jesus made:

> **But the Comforter, *which is* the Holy Ghost, whom the Father will send in my name, he shall teach you all things, and bring all things to your remembrance, whatsoever I have said unto you.**
>
> **(John 14:26)**

By the time Peter finished his sermon, an impromptu altar call had ensued as the listeners asked what they should do. That's when Peter provided the answer to those riddles.

> **"Then Peter said unto them, Repent, and be baptized every one of you in the name of Jesus Christ for the re-mission of sins, and ye shall receive the gift of the Holy Ghost."**
>
> **(Acts 2:38)**

Two analogies come to mind concerning the three-step process to complete the Birthing Equation that Peter provided. First, I think of Moses, who was permitted only to see the Promised Land because he didn't follow all of God's commandments. I liken that to being born again in John 3:3. He was forbidden to enter, but at least he could see what He forfeited.[178]

To extend this analogy to today, I compare it to travel. I enjoy looking at images of scenic places worldwide, but there's nothing like visiting or living in those places. Without a passport, I would have never gained entrance to South Africa. Without citizenship, I could not enjoy all the benefits South African citizens carry. More importantly, my time there had an expiration date. At that time, I had to forfeit the benefits I previously enjoyed.

The second analogy is when babies are born. The birthing process begins with labor when the baby decides it is ready to be born and begins its descent through the birth canal. The baby is alive but transitioning from depending on the mother's oxygen to independent breathing. Next is the delivery. The baby then exits the womb and passes through the birth canal to enter the world. Yet, the baby will not survive unless the final step is complete, which is taking that first breath. Once that first breath has been taken, the baby has full access to all the benefits of the location where the birth took place. Death will occur if the baby doesn't breathe.

Based on Peter's exhortation, the Birthing Equation has officially been solved:

	Birthing Stage	Natural Birth	Spiritual Birth
	Born Again (Repentance)	Labor	(Seeing the promised Land, i.e., Kingdom of God
+	Born Of Water (Baptism)	Delivery	(Passport to the Promised Land)
+	Born Of Spirit (Other Tongues)	First Breath	(Full citizenship in the Promised Land with full access to all its' benefits)
=	*New Birth/Kingdom Citizen (Riddle Solved)*		

If you want to enjoy full citizenship of the Kingdom of God, apply the New Birth Equation in your life that:

→ Enables you to harness the power of discernment,
→ tap into all other spiritual gifts, and
→ exponentially increase your ability to maximize the principles listed in this book.

I echo what Jesus said. You ***must*** be born again. If you haven't already, I encourage you to complete the process.

Key Takeaways:

→ Your presumption must line up with the scripture in its entirety. Thus, never attempt to manipulate scripture to justify your hypothesis.

→ Scriptural evidence of the infilling of the Holy Spirit is speaking in tongues. Tongues is a prayer language in which one prays for God's will purely.

→ Just as natural birth is a process that includes labor, delivery, and breathing, the entire new birth experience is a process consisting of repentance, baptism, and Holy Spirit infilling.

Reflections:

→ Can you think of a time that you subscribed to a belief based on misinterpreted scripture? What was your process of discovering the correct interpretation?

→ How do you distinguish the difference between seeing and entering the Kingdom of God?

→ Reflect on your new-birth experience. Have you received your passport or citizenship into the Kingdom of God?

Prayer (For those who cannot see the Kingdom of God yet):

Heavenly Father, I thank You for the sacrifice You made by sending Your Son, Jesus, to become sin so that I can be set free from sin. Forgive me for my sins. Wash me clean and make me new. I surrender my life fully to You. Please lead me to God-fearing, Bible-believing people of God who will teach me how to immerse myself in Your Word, Your will, and Your ways. Send me to people who are willing to surrender their ideologies and theories to the truth of Your Holy Word. I want to Know You, Father. Please, show me Your Glory, Jesus Christ, and fill me with Your sweet Holy Spirit. Thank You for Your forgiveness, Your Spirit, and your guidance, in Jesus' name. AMEN!

Prayer (For those who hold passports to visit the Kingdom of God):

Sweet Savior, thank You for revealing Your prescription for salvation. Thank You for the grace to move me into repentance. Thank You for cleansing my sins through baptism. Thank You for sending the Holy Spirit to earth to comfort, lead and guide me. You promised that You would pour out Your Spirit on All Flesh. I ask You to pour Your Spirit into my flesh as well. I invite Your holy presence into the atmosphere as I worship You for Your goodness, mercy, and grace. Fill me with the power of Your Spirit as You did for the multitudes on the day of Pentecost, and continue to do today. I surrender my tongue to You as I praise You. As I open my mouth to speak praises to You, I praise You by faith for pouring your Spirit into mine. I trust You to be the Great Promise Keeper, and I thank You for filling my spirit with Your precious Holy Ghost, in Jesus' name. AMEN!

After praying this prayer, drown out all distractions and begin to lift your voice in praise to the Lord God Almighty.

Prayer (For Kingdom Citizens):

My great and wondrous Lord, God, and King, I bless You for granting me citizenship in Your Kingdom. I thank You for all the benefits that Your Kingdom bestows upon me. I thank You for completing the birthing process in my life, and I bless You for the flame of Your Spirit burning within me. Jesus, I invite You to ignite Your flame within me so that I can activate and demonstrate every gift at my disposal. Use me as an ambassador to usher others into Your Kingdom, not just for a brief visit but for permanent residency. Kindle in me a deeper passion for more intimacy with You, in Jesus' Name. AMEN!

Chapter 15

CONCLUSION OF THE MATTER

*Let us hear the conclusion of the whole matter: Fear God,
and keep his commandments: for this is the whole duty of
man. For God shall bring every work into judgment, with every
secret thing, whether it be good, or whether it be evil.
(Ecclesiastes 12:13-14)*

*And it came to pass, that when all our enemies heard thereof, and all the
heathen that were about us saw these things, they were much cast down in
their own eyes: for they perceived that this work was wrought of our God.
(Nehemiah 6:16)*

Review

This book has unveiled ten principles that Nehemiah exhibited while rebuilding the walls and city of Jerusalem. By combining all ten principles, Nehemiah was able to complete the project in an astounding 52 days. Let's briefly summarize each principle to ensure that we become better leaders ourselves:

1. *The Establishment Principle* introduces us to God's requirements for "hiring" employees. While we like to rely on qualifications, God establishes those whom He chooses, then equips them for the task at hand.

2. *The Origin Principle* leads us straight to the heart of God. This principle dictates that we place God as our top priority. Before embarking on any venture, our first step is to seek Him and all His righteousness first.

3. *The Prioritization Principle* reveals the significance of structure through the blueprint that God used in the creation story.

4. *The Model Principle* teaches us how to set an example through our lifestyles for others to follow.

5. *The Lowly Principle* shows us the value of humility and reveals the requirement for exaltation.

6. *The Servant Principle* explains the importance of meekness.

7. *The Unity Principle* – Well, it speaks for itself. Unity is required to complete any task assigned to a group in peace successfully.

8. *The Discussion Principle* delves into how we communicate, and provides strategies for enhancing communication skills.

9. *The Calendar Principle* provides the importance for utilizing the time God has given us wisely, and strategies for time management

10. *The Knowledge Principle* reveals how powerful words are, and teaches us how to use our words wisely. This principle also emphasizes the importance of discernment.

So now, without further ado, I will attempt to wrap these principles up in a tidy box and put a bow on them like this:

God *ESTABLISHED* Jesus, the *ORIGIN* of our salvation, to set us free from the bondage of sin. Jesus made us His first *PRIORITY* and *MODELED* for us the royal behavior that is pleasing to Him. Humbling Himself, Jesus became a *LOWLY SERVANT* so that we could gain *KNOWLEDGE* of the power we have in Him. He desired that we be in *UNITY* with Him just as He is with the Father. He *DISCUSSED* all of this with His disciples when He told them about the place He is preparing for us. While it isn't on any human Calendar, He has an appointed time in His *CALENDAR* to return and reunite us with Him, and so shall we ever be with the Lord. **AMEN!**

Let us learn from Nehemiah. Let us lead the way God desires us to lead. Let us focus our efforts on seeking the Kingdom of God first and allowing God to add "all these things" to us as a body, as groups, as colleagues, as teammates, as a nation, as a kingdom. Let us allow Nehemiah's principles to become a factor in our lives.

ENDNOTES

Chapter 1

1   "Leaders." Merriam-Webster. Merriam-Webster. Accessed May 17, 2021. https://www.merriam-webster.com/dictionary/leaders.

2   "Principle." Merriam-Webster. Merriam-Webster. Accessed May 17, 2021. https://www.merriam-webster.com/dictionary/principle.

3   Newton, Isaac, Andrew Motte, William Davis, William Emerson, and John Machin. The Mathematical Principles of Natural Philosophy. London: Printed for Sherwood, Neely, and Jones, 1819.

4   "Why Is There No Gravity in Space?" Science Questions with Surprising Answers. Accessed May 17, 2021. https://wtamu.edu/~cbaird/sq/2012/12/18/why-is-there-no-gravity-in-space/.

5   Meyers, Rick. E-Sword. Vers. 10.4. Franklin, TN: www.e-sword.net, 2000-2019. Computer software. International Standard Bible Encyclopedia, Nehemiah 1:11

6   "City+Walls: Manners+&+Customs - Resources for Ancient Biblical Studies." Ark of the Covenant - Bible History Online. Accessed May 17, 2021. https://www.bible-history.com/links.php?-cat=39&sub=433&cat_name=Manners%2B%26%2BCustoms&sub-cat_name=City%2BWalls.

7   Nehemiah 6:15

8   1 Corinthians 12:12-28

9   Cf. Genesis 41:32; Deuteronomy 19:15; Job 33:14-17; Matthew 18:15-16; 2 Corinthians 13:1.

Chapter 2

10   Isaiah 55:8-9

11 Nehemiah 1:1, 11
12 Cupbearer. Accessed May 18, 2021. https://www.jewishvirtuallibrary.org/cupbearer.
13 Judges 6:12-14
14 Hebrews 4:12
15 Clance, Pauline Rose, and Suzanne Ament Imes. "The Imposter Phenomenon in High Achieving Women: Dynamics and Therapeutic Intervention." Psychotherapy: Theory, Research & Practice 15, no. 3 (1978): 241–47. https://doi.org/10.1037/h0086006.
16 Judges chapter 11
17 Isaiah 55:9
18 I completed the Christian International Authorized Instructor Program in 2001.
19 Ester 4:14

Chapter 3

20 Nehemiah 1:4, AMP
21 Or, give favor
22 Meyers, Rick. E-Sword. Vers. 12.1 Franklin, TN: www.e-sword.net, 2000-2019. Computer software. Jammieson, Faucet and Brown Commentary, Nehemiah 2:2
23 1 John 4:18, AMP
24 James 1:22
25 See Nehemiah 2:5-8
26 Jeremiah 29:11
27 John 10:10
28 Genesis 6
29 Psalm 37:23
30 "What Is Marketplace Ministry?" Christian Faith at Work, June 14, 2017. https://www.christianfaithatwork.com/what-is-marketplace-ministry/.
31 "Structure." Merriam-Webster. Merriam-Webster. Accessed May 18, 2021. https://www.merriam-webster.com/dictionary/structure.
32 Genesis 1:2-8, NIV
33 Genesis 1:9, NIV

34 Proverbs 8:29

35 Nehemiah 2:16-18

36 See Jeremiah 29:11 and Proverbs 16:3

37 Meyers, Rick. E-Sword. Vers. 12.1 Franklin, TN: www.e-sword.net, 2000-2019. Computer software. Hastings' Dictionary of the Bible, Sanballat

38 Nehemiah 4:13

39 II Corinthians 10:4

40 Cf. Job 1:6-19; 1 Kings 22.

41 Meyers, Rick. E-Sword. Vers. 12.1 Franklin, TN: www.e-sword.net, 2000-2019. Computer software. Hastings' Dictionary of the Bible, Tobiah

42 Nehemiah 6:7, NLT

43 Proverbs 18:21

44 John 11:41-43

45 John 14:12

46 Cf. Joshua 10:12-13.

47 Matthew 16:19

48 Ibid.

49 Hebrews 5:14

50 A cell group is a small group of like-minded Christians who meet together during the week to study, worship, and pray. Some are formed through local churches, while others are formed by like-minded Christians seeking growth and accountability. They are known by a variety of names including, home groups, small groups, fellowship groups, and care groups.

51 Philippians 4:6-7

52 "The Great Telecom Implosion." Princeton University. The Trustees of Princeton University. Accessed May 18, 2021. https://www.princeton.edu/~starr/articles/articles02/Starr-TelecomImplosion-9-02.htm.; "The Whistleblower And The CEO In the Lucent Scandal, the Ex-Boss Will Walk. The Woman Who Accused Him Is Now an SEC Target. And Guess Who's Paying the Penalty? Owners like You." CNNMoney. Cable News Network, July 7, 2003. https://money.cnn.com/magazines/fortune/fortune_archive/2003/07/07/345538/index.htm.

53 Psalm 37:25; Philippians 4:13

54 2 Thessalonians 3:10, WEB; 1 Samuel 15:22, ESV

55 What Does it Mean To Be "In the World but Not of It"? (n.d.). Crosswalk. com. Retrieved March 11, 2021, from https://www.crosswalk.com/faith/ spiritual-life/what-does-it-mean-to-be-in-the-world-but-not-of-it.html

56 Cf. Meyers, Rick. E-Sword. Vers. 12.1 Franklin, TN: www.e-sword.net, 2000-2019. Computer software. Adam Clarke's Commentary of the Bible, Luke 6:38, "Almost all ancient nations wore long, wide, and loose garments; and when about to carry any thing which their hands could not contain, they used a fold of their robe in nearly the same way as women here use their aprons."

57 Cf. Matthew 14:28-31.

58 James 2:20

59 Matthew 6:33

Chapter 4

60 Romans 14:17

61 Isaiah 64:6

62 Psalm 37:4

63 Philippians 4:6, NIV

64 Popik, Barry. "Barry Popik." The Big Apple. Accessed July 18, 2021. https://www.barrypopik.com/index.php/new_york_city/ entry/how_do_you_eat_an_elephant#:~:text=The%20proverb%20 became%20popular%20in,published%20in%20a%201945%20book.

65 Meyers, Rick. E-Sword. Vers. 12.1 Franklin, TN: www.e-sword.net, 2000-2019. Computer software. Fausset's Bible Dictionary, Hanani

66 See Ruth chapters 2-3

67 Exodus 33:11

68 2 Kings 2:9-12

69 Cf. Matthew 25:14-30.

70 Source Unknown

71 Cf. Genesis 22:1-14

72 The Bible Journey | 25. The Israelites journey from Egypt to Mt Sinai. (n.d.). Www.thebiblejourney.org. https://www.thebiblejourney.org/biblejourney2/2 5-the-israelites-journey-from-egypt-to-mt-sinai/

Chapter 5

73 "Model." Merriam-Webster. Merriam-Webster. Accessed May 20, 2021. https://www.merriam-webster.com/dictionary/model.

74 Nehemiah 2:12-17

75 ABC News. ABC News Network. Accessed May 20, 2021. https://abcnews.go.com/US/sexual-encounters-allegedly-everyday-thing-students-california-preschool/story?id=18402570.

76 Colossians 1:27

77 Cf. 1 Kings chapters 17-19, 21.

78 Cf. 2 Kings 2:9.

79 1 Kings 19:21

80 "Minister." Dictionary.com. Dictionary.com. Accessed May 20, 2021. https://www.dictionary.com/browse/minister.

81 Cf. Numbers 12:3; Exodus 33:1, AMP; Exodus 33:20, John 1:18, 6:46, 1 Timothy 6:16, 1 John 4:12.

82 Cf. Numbers 20:7-12; Deuteronomy 31:1-8.

83 Cf. Joshua chapter 6.

84 Cf. 1 Thessalonians 4:11-12; Nehemiah 1:4-11; 2:9-15; 4:1-14.

85 "The Triple Filter Test - Is It True? Is It Good? Is It Useful? > Learning Architects." Learning Architects, December 30, 2019. https://www.learningarchitects.com/the-triple-filter-test-is-it-true-is-it-good-is-it-useful/#:~:text=It%20is%20called%20.

86 Philippians 2:5

Chapter 6

87 Cf. Hebrews 12:2; Revelation chapter 5.

88 Philippians 2:8

89 Galatians 3:13

90 Cf; Ephesians 3:1-11; "The Dispensation of Grace." Berean Bible Society, November 11, 2019. https://www.bereanbiblesociety.org/part-1-the-dispensation-of-grace-mystery-or-prophecy/.

91 Hebrews 12:2

92 Nehemiah 2:6

93 Cf. Nehemiah 1:5-11; Cupbearer. Accessed May 20, 2021. https://www.jew-ishvirtuallibrary.org/cupbearer.

94 Nehemiah 5:14-15

95 1 John 2:16

96 Cf. Isaiah 14:12-17, Ezekiel 28:14; Luke 10:18.

97 Ezekiel 28:12-18

98 Cf. Ephesians 2:2; 2 Corinthians 4:4; Job 1:6.

99 I have elected not to capitalize satan's name as I esteem him worthy of such honor.

100 John 13:3-11

101 "The Bible Journey | 1. The World of the New Testament Journeys." The Bible Journey. Accessed October 13, 2021. https://thebiblejourney.org/biblejourney 1/1-the-world-of-the-new-testament-journeys-b/.

102 Matthew 27:11-14

103 Matthew 26:67; 27:27-44

104 Luke 22:50-52

105 Proverbs 18:16

106 Humble | Meaning of Humble by Lexico. (n.d.). Lexico Dictionaries | English. https://www.lexico.com/definition/humble

107 MEEK | Definition of MEEK by Oxford Dictionary on Lexico.com also meaning of MEEK. (n.d.). Lexico Dictionaries | English. Retrieved April 4, 2021, from https://www.lexico.com/definition/meek

108 Numbers 12:3

109 Philippians 3:8, ESV

110 2 Corinthians 5:21

Chapter 7

111 Horwitt, Arnold, Gene Nelson, and Sidney Sheldon. I Dream of Jeannie. United States: NBC Television Network, 1965.

112 Source Unknown

113 Isaiah 14:12-14

114 Proverbs 16:18

115 Exodus chapter 18

116 Cf. Ruth 2:22-23; 3:1-6, 4:17 and Matthew 1:1, 5, 16.

Chapter 8

117 Brady, Nicholas, Nahum Tate, William Burkitt, and John Veneer. The Book of Common Prayer. London: Thos. Kelly, 1839.

118 Revelation 12:10

119 Philippians 2:2, ESV

120 I Corinthians 1:10

121 Acts 15:36-41

122 Acts 1:14-26

123 Numbers 27:1-11, Numbers 36:1-10

124 Cf. Romans 12:2.

125 Acts chapter 2

126 Cf. Acts 5:12-19; 16:25-31.

Chapter 9

127 Left foot of fellowship is a play on the expression, "Right hand of fellowship" which refers to a tradition in which the pastor extends his/her right hand to the new member to officially welcome that person as a part of the local assembly.

128 Cf. Joshua Chapter 7

129 Romans 12:3

130 1 Corinthians 5:5, GW

131 James 5:19-20, GW

132 Acts 15:36-40, AMP

133 Cf. Acts 13:13; Meyers, Rick. E-Sword. Vers. 12.1 Franklin, TN: www.e-sword.net, 2000-2019. Computer software. Dr. Kretzmann's Popular Commentary, Acts 15:36-41.

134 Cf. Colossians 4:10-11, 2 Timothy 4:11.

135 Meyers, Rick. E-Sword. Vers. 12.1 Franklin, TN: www.e-sword.net, 2000-2019. Computer software. John Gills Exposition of the Entire Bible, Acts 15:37

Chapter 10

136 Cf. Genesis chapter 1.

137 Romans 4:17

138 Proverbs 18:21

139 Proverbs 12:13, ERV

140 1 Corinthians 10:23

141 Ephesians. 4:29

142 Psalm 141:3, ESV

143 Acts 11:4

144 Acts 14:17

145 Overlearning, Choking, Einstellung, Chunking, and Interleaving. Coursera. org. Coursera Online Course. Accessed July 30, 2021. Course notes for "Overlearning-choking-einstellung-chunking-and-interleaving" by Deep Teaching Solutions

146 Warren, Shellie R., Shellie R. Warren, and Shellie R. WarrenLife Coach Shellie R Warren is an author. "10 Most Common Reasons for Divorce." Marriage Advice - Expert Marriage Tips & Advice, January 14, 2021. https:// www.marriage.com/advice/divorce/10-most-common-reasons-for-divorce/.

147 Cain, Fraser. "How Long Does It Take Sunlight to Reach the Earth?" Phys. org - News and Articles on Science and Technology. Phys.org, April 15, 2013. https://phys.org/news/2013-04-sunlight-earth.amp.

148 Nehemiah 1:4

Chapter 11

149 Cf. Nehemiah 1:1; 2:1; "The Circle of a Year." The Jerusalem Post | JPost.com. Accessed May 20, 2021. https://www.jpost.com/israel-news/ the-circle-of-a-year-603008.

150 2 Chronicles 33:1-11

151 Matthew 25:1-12

152 Matthew 25:15, ERV

153 "Faultline: Earthquake Engineering." Exploratorium. Accessed May 20, 2021. https://www.exploratorium.edu/faultline/damage/building.html.

Chapter 12

154 Nehemiah 7:1-2
155 Meyers, Rick. E-Sword. Vers. 10.4. Franklin, TN: www.e-sword.net, 2000-2019. Computer software. Adam Clarke's Commentary of the Bible, Nehemiah 7:2 (c)
156 Nehemiah 6:10-14
157 John 4:1-29
158 Cf. Ezekiel 17-21; chapter 33; Amos 3:7; Luke 21:25, 34-36; Matthew 24:37-39.

Chapter 13

159 Acts 1:6-11
160 Acts 2:3-4
161 Cf. Hebrews 4:14-16; 7:25; Romans 8:34.
162 Cf. Leviticus chapter 16; Hebrews 4:14-16.
163 Cf. 1 Corinthians 14:4; Hebrews 5:14.
164 1 Corinthians 12:7, ESV
165 2 Timothy 1:6
166 Meyers, Rick. E-Sword. Vers. 10.4. Franklin, TN: www.e-sword.net, 2000-2019. Computer software. Mounce Concise Greek-English Dictionary, G329, ἀναζωπυρέω

Chapter 14

167 Cf. 2 Samuel 9:8; 2 Kings 8:13; Matthew 15:26-27, Philippians 3:2.
168 Cf. Meyers, Rick. E-Sword. Vers. 10.4. Franklin, TN: www.e-sword.net, 2000-2019. Computer software. Treasury of Scriptural Knowledge, Philippians 3:2; Meyers, Rick. E-Sword. Vers. 10.4. Franklin, TN: www.e-sword.net, 2000-2019. Computer software. Mounce Concise Greek-English Dictionary, Matthew 15:26, Philippians 3:2.
169 Mozaffarian, Dariush, and David S. Ludwig. "The 2015 US Dietary Guidelines – Ending the 35% Limit on Total Dietary Fat." JAMA. U.S.

   National Library of Medicine. Accessed May 26, 2021. https://www.ncbi.
   nlm.nih.gov/pmc/articles/PMC6129189/.

170 1 Corinthians 13:9-12

171 "The Indulgences Controversy of Martin Luther." Encyclopædia Britannica.
   Encyclopædia Britannica, inc. Accessed May 20, 2021. https://www.britan-
   nica.com/biography/Martin-Luther/The-indulgences-controversy.

172 Howell, Kenneth. "Aren't We Saved by Faith Alone?" Catholic Answers.
   Catholic Answers, May 2, 2019. https://www.catholic.com/magazine/
   print-edition/arent-we-saved-by-faith-alone.

173 1 Peter 1:8

174 John 14:15-18

175 Acts 1:8

176 Acts 2:3, NIV

177 Cf. Acts 2:1-4; 10:44-46; 19:6.

178 Deuteronomy 32:48-52

AUTHOR RESOURCES

Most people do not realize that the only thing a leader needs to lead is a follower. *The Nehemiah Factors (TNF)* is written for leaders of all capacities, from the minister to the mother to the corporate executive.

The book of Nehemiah contains a treasure-trove of principles that, if implemented, will elevate the leadership style of your team from mediocre to highly effective. *The Nehemiah Factors* highlights those principles and provide practical application. This prose is an excellent training tool for new and seasoned leaders alike.

In addition to this book, the author conducts *The Nehemiah Factors* online training classes. If you are interested in hosting a *TNF* class for your team, please e-mail us at TNF@globalgrowthpublishing.org.